CRISIS IN BETHLEHEM

This book is dedicated to those loyal
Bethlehem workers who helped make steel the
might of America, especially to those who
challenged the comfortable status quo, and to
all those who now strive to save the company.

CRISIS IN BETHLEHEM

BIG STEEL'S STRUGGLE TO SURVIVE

JOHN STROHMEYER

UNIVERSITY OF PITTSBURGH PRESS

Pittsburgh and London

Published by the University of Pittsburgh Press, Pittsburgh, Pa., 15260
First published in the United States of America by
Adler & Adler Publishers, Inc., 1986
Published by Penguin Books, 1987
University of Pittsburgh Press edition, 1994

10 9 8 7 6 5 4 3

Library of Congress Cataloging-in-Publication Data

Strohmeyer, John, 1924–
    Crisis in Bethlehem: big steel's struggle to survive / by John Strohmeyer.–
University of Pittsburgh Press ed.
        p.   cm.
    Originally published: Bethesda, Md.: Adler & Adler, 1986. With new preface.
    Includes index.
    ISBN 0-8229-5811-2 (alk. paper)
    1. Bethlehem Steel Corporation–History. 2. Steel industry and trade–United
States–History. 3. Trade-unions–Iron and steel workers–Pennsylvania–
Bethlehem–History. 4. Iron and steel workers–Pennsylvania–Bethlehem–
History. I. Title.
HD9519.B4S87   1994
338.7′669142′0974822–dc20   94-13505   CIP

Contents

Acknowledgments

I thought of writing this book many times during my years as editor of the *Globe-Times* in Bethlehem, Pennsylvania. However, I could not have left the daily deadlines without the support of the Alicia Patterson Foundation. At age 60, I was awarded a 1984–85 Alicia Patterson Fellowship, a prize the foundation normally bestows upon the brightest young minds of an emerging generation of journalists. I am grateful for their faith in my project and for the warm encouragement of Cathy Trost, editor of the Alicia Patterson Foundation Reporter.

The pulse of this book comes from interviews with more than 100 people—from steel-mill workers on the plant floor, to top executives in the corporate tower, plus their families. I also went beyond the industry to interview academics, union leaders, and foundation experts at research-oriented think tanks. Nearly all consented to give their viewpoints and experiences on tape. My thanks to all of them, and particularly to Joe Mangan, a founding member of the steel union movement in Bethlehem, who helped round up the others; to my friend Lewis Field, whose devotion to steelmaking and experience in developing it into an industrial art form, provided me with much technical counsel; and to Donald Trautlein, former Bethlehem Steel chairman, who set an example of candor and gave me access to many sources in the executive suites.

Acknowledgments

I prepared this book at Moravian College, which provided me with an office at Hamilton Hall—just a few steps away from its excellent Reeves Library, where Thomas J. Minor's staff accommodated my every wish. At Bethlehem Steel, Henry H. Von Spreckelsen, manager of corporate communications, patiently fulfilled many requests for pertinent company materials, and Darla, Barbara, and Marie at the Schwab Library cheerfully dug out documents even after the library staff was cut to an austerity level. Louise Grow, my talented former secretary and librarian at the *Globe-Times,* pulled files for me at the newspaper morgue with a dedication I am not sure I deserved.

Finally, a word of appreciation for the help of my family. My brother, Joe, a Bethlehem Steel employee, gave me a lifetime of inside impressions at the mill until he died of cancer at the age of 56. My son, John, regaled our dinner table with his experiences at the ingot mold until the dust and the din convinced him to return to college. And above all, I am most indebted to my wife, Nancy, a former newsperson and book-publishing employee. She challenged facts and assumptions, edited awkward phrases, and offered important suggestions on filling information gaps, insisting that I aim for the highest standards in our truly mutual pursuit of history.

Bethlehem, Pa.
March 3, 1986

What did the integrated steel industry learn from the mistakes that brought on the severe trauma of the 1980s? Not much, if you look at the profit sheets of the 1990s. Domestic steelmakers lost $3.1 billion during the years 1991–92. While several of the more diversified companies started showing a profit in 1993, Bethlehem Steel, the number-two producer and still the purest and the least diversified of the big American steelmakers, continued losing, ending the year with a loss of $266.3 million.

However, the heavy red ink during the early 1990s obscures several positive changes that had been occurring. The steel industry had posted profits in 1988 and 1989, showing signs that the big producers who seemed to have lost their way had finally found their compasses. However, the persistent recession that began in 1990 eroded those gains, dropping prices to lowest levels in a decade.

At Bethlehem Steel, Walter Williams, who succeeded Donald Trautlein as chairman in 1986, did appear to be getting Bethlehem back on track by accelerating the cost-cutting started by his embattled predecessor. He sold off the corporation's nonproductive and costly peripheral operations—the quarries, the coal mines, the jet planes, the ore boats, and even a plastics plant, which represented Bethlehem's modest foray into diversification.

"Then we went and got a new revolver," as Williams put

it. He zeroed in on costs of production, modernizing the viable plants and getting rid of the others. He went to Lackawanna, New York, to close a bar mill that he once helped design. He put the entire Johnstown, Pennsylvania, plant up for sale. He warned the union that the hot metal operations at the home plant in Bethlehem were in jeopardy unless work rule concessions were forthcoming. He gave workers in the plants a greater role in decisions but notified them that the bottom line was to meet production costs of the competition, including the new minimills which are now turning out sheets and plates, once the exclusive domain of the integrated mills.

Eighty percent of Bethlehem Steel henceforth will come from two facilities distant from Bethlehem, Pennsylvania. The Burns Harbor plant in Indiana, the last major steel mill built in the United States, has emerged as the flagship. It is close to its main customers, the midwest automobile plants, and Williams claims the United Steelworkers Union there has helped the company make it one of the most efficient steel plants in the country, attaining productivity of three man hours per ton versus the five and a half hours per ton which seems to be the standard for the industry covering all steel products. The second designated mill of the future is at Sparrows Point, Maryland. Because of its excellent harbor location, this plant has received over one billion dollars of modernization over the last ten years, gearing it to low cost, premier products that will compete with minimills and unsubsidized steel.

Having set the course for Bethlehem's survival, Williams stepped down as chairman late in 1992 and was replaced by Curtis H. Barnette, the corporation's chief counsel. While continuing William's cost-cutting plans, Barnette has been working on another agenda to save steelmaking. He has joined other steelmakers in bringing ninety-four individual lawsuits against twenty-one countries—Japan, Canada, and most of Europe and South America—seeking redress for illegal dumping of flat rolled steel products. A total of seventy-two of these cases were cleared to proceed at the onset of 1993, but the industry won only a partial victory. The cases lost, involving about half of the tonnage in dispute, have been appealed. The inevitable delays in litigation make it unlikely that government help in the form of tariffs or quotas may soon give the industry the relief it wished from the dumping that it has sought since the voluntary quota agreements expired during the Bush administration.

Meanwhile, labor relations with the United Steelworkers Union have improved. The union's hard stance on work rules began to melt as plant after plant closed across the country. Since 1980, steel employment fell from 391,000 workers to 183,000. Stunned union local leaders, with few exceptions, resigned themselves to the inevitable, fighting mainly to protect rights of the displaced. With contracts reopening at at least four major steel firms in 1993, the tough threats of strikes were noticeably absent from the union's international headquarters. Instead, its national leaders said they would seek innovative agreements with steelmakers, including ways to cut work forces and relax stringent work rules. "The industry has needs and the American economy has needs," USW president Lynn Williams declared.

However, big steel's progress in its struggle to survive offers little comfort to the steel towns that America used to know. They will never be the same. In Bethlehem, the steel firm that used to provide 21,000 well-paying jobs there when I became editor of the *Globe-Times* in 1956 now employs about 4,500 workers. This has changed not only the economy but the character of Bethlehem, and one of these changes was particularly painful for me. In 1991, the *Globe-Times,* once a thriving paper of 38,000 subscribers, was sold to the Thomson newspaper chain which closed the plant, dismissed the workers, and merged the masthead with its paper in Easton, Pennsylvania. Now, Bethlehem, a distinctive city of 75,000 people which traces its origins to 1741, does not have a daily voice of its own.

Preface

Late in January 1994, Bethlehem suffered the ultimate indignity. The steel company announced that despite union concessions it has been forced to close down the hot metal steelmaking operations in Bethlehem. Those roaring blast furnaces which gave Bethlehem Steel its life and its name in 1904 will be silenced forever. By 1996, when the phase-out is complete, 2,000 more jobs will be lost. The steelmaking skills passed down by generations of Bethlehem families will be useless.

The city reacted with shock. The stock market was delighted. Heavy buying sent Bethlehem Steel shares soaring to a year's new high. The saga of Bethlehem becomes a case study of the tumultuous, often insensitive, profit-driven changes occurring in this nation's once impregnable industries. For the city, its once-booming steelmaking complex is destined to become a museum, complete with guides to show how men of brawn and brains once made the mighty beams that support the structures which grace American skylines.

JOHN STROHMEYER
January 30, 1994

ONE afternoon in the late summer of 1985, Richard Lynn, a thirty-eight-year-old steelworker, gathered his eight-year-old twin sons around him on a settee in the sun porch of their Bethlehem, Pennsylvania, home.

"Boys, the family luck has run out," he told them. "You better get an education because there's not going to be a job like I had or your grandfather had. We're not sure there's going to be a Bethlehem Steel company."

For a man whose family had a proud record of five generations with Bethlehem Steel, it was a bitter legacy for Richard Lynn to pass on. But the decline in the American steel industry is changing family patterns far beyond Bethlehem. The problems are changing the face of industrial America.

In the space of forty years, this basic industry has gone from a powerful monolith virtually invulnerable to society's ills to an ailing weakling. The liquidation of steel manufacturing is uprooting many thousands of once-secure American workers and undermining the fiscal health of their communities. It is creating traumatic confrontations between labor and management. It poses difficult government policy decisions and threatens national security. It confounds administrations, tests congresses, and splits political parties. And it is no temporary phenomenon.

The rise and fall of steel—and now its struggle to survive—has been well reported statistically. In 1946, the industry figures portrayed an image of national strength. An estimated 85 percent of all manufactured goods in the United States contained steel in one form or another, and 40 percent of all wage earners in the country owed their livelihoods to steel, directly or indirectly. The might of nations was measured by steel production, and the United States was the mightiest of them all because it could roll more than 90 million tons of steel ingots a year, far beyond the capability of any other country.

Now, forty years later, steel industry statistics portray an image of national debilitation—more than 250,000 jobs lost forever, more than 30 million tons of capacity wiped out as aging facilities are shut down never to reopen, and one-fourth of the domestic market captured by aggressive foreign nations with newer plants and lower wage rates. A final demoralizing statistic: the American steel industry has lost $7.25 billion during the four years since it began its plunge in 1981.

However, the sweep of this story goes much farther. Beyond the statistics are the multitudes who devoted their lives to steel—the laborers and craftsmen, the brain trusts and union bosses, the many levels of support workers. They ran the corporate offices, manufactured the steel, and made the fateful decisions that once gave such predictability to life and now bring so much uncertainty.

For many, a job in steel was the achievement of the American dream. The industry was the melting pot for hundreds of thousands of immigrants with willing muscles and a strong work ethic. They supplied the brawn for the entrepreneurs who built steelmaking empires. The empires in turn spawned corporate tycoons, many of them extraordinary men in industry but many also shamelessly greedy about their personal worth; they grew so smug that they became oblivious to what was happening in the world around them.

Then there are the militant and politically ambitious union leaders. They rescued the American steelworker from primitive working conditions and peon pay in the dirty, ear-shattering, and often dangerous shops. They challenged the companies with nationwide strikes that regularly disrupted the economy, gaining the highest wages, longest vacations, and greatest number of featherbedding work rules in American manufacturing. Now the union leaders fight to cling to those benefits while watching their steel mills lose competitiveness, shrink operations, and discharge the workers whose jobs the unions were founded to protect.

On the periphery of the steel story is a diverse cast carrying the banner of government. Four American presidents personally intervened in attempts to bring order to this often-troubled basic industry. To avoid the national shock of a steel strike, they in turn seized the mills, assumed seats at the bargaining table, lashed out at inflationary price increases, even locked industry and labor negotiators in the White House.

Less visible, but wielding profound power, were the government bureaucrats. They demanded that the American steel companies comply with the world's severest environmental controls, strictest safety standards, and most demanding minority hiring and promoting quotas. The bureaucrats acted, meanwhile, in the name of a government that persisted in maintaining, for its steel industry, the world's most repressive tax depreciation policies.

As editor of the Bethlehem *Globe-Times* in the twenty-eight years between 1956 and 1984, I watched from a front-row seat as the steel industry went from boom to brink. Bethlehem is the headquarters of the Bethlehem Steel Corporation, the nation's No. 2 steel producer until 1985. Its clang and roar were the life sounds of my town. I have emotional ties to this story. Friends and relatives, including a son and a brother, worked at the company, and I knew some of those who died there. But the reason for using Bethlehem Steel for this systemic account is far more than personal. The company was an archetype of corporate success.

Starting at the turn of the century with a small mill on the banks of the Lehigh River in eastern Pennsylvania, Bethlehem

Steel became an industrial colossus of steel mills, shipyards, railroads, coal mines, and mineral interests stretching across the continent. When, in response to Pearl Harbor, the country's industrial might was called upon for the largest war effort in history, Bethlehem quickly geared its mills to turn out millions of tons of steel for tanks, guns, and bombs. From 1939 to 1946, the company built 1,121 naval and merchant ships and repaired 3,800 more vessels, a record unmatched by any private shipbuilder in the world.

Having helped save America in war, Bethlehem Steel built much of the country in peace, adding a massive, coordinated force of technicians, erectors, and researchers to back up its rapidly expanding steel manufacturing capability. National landmarks extending from the George Washington Bridge to the Golden Gate testify to Bethlehem's engineering and construction expertise. It had a large role in shaping the skylines of the major cities, supplying the steel and erecting such buildings as the Waldorf-Astoria in New York, the Merchandise Mart in Chicago, and the National Gallery of Art in Washington. The nation's missile silos, among other national security installations, today are testimony to the company's technology as well as its steelmaking capacity.

In its near collapse, Bethlehem Steel stands out again as an archetype, this time as a company struggling for survival in America's changing economic landscape. In 1980, Bethlehem abandoned its traditional route of succession to power by picking Donald Trautlein, an accountant, whose lack of steelmaking know-how defied the public conception of a steel industry leader. Trautlein promptly did what none of his predecessors dared to do. He fired thousands of workers, closed down entire plants, sold off others, cut pay, and eliminated perks. His merciless actions in the name of survival created waves of societal traumas.

Meanwhile, the American steelworker became an archetype of the embattled industrial union worker in this changing economic scenario. He was forced to swallow his pride and put old antagonisms aside. "Concessionary bargaining" became the new battleground. When confronted with the choice of concessions or shutdown, the response at first was, "Hell, no, Bethlehem has too much invested to shut us down." But when steel plants did shut down and jobs vanished, union attitudes changed. Whether they are changing significantly enough to save Bethlehem Steel and, in fact, the distressed industry, is not yet evident.

All the modern dilemmas of a union's relationship to a company are being played out in steel's attempt to save itself. An encouraging story is found in Weirton, West Virginia, where independent union employees at Weirton Steel abandoned old adversarial scripts and actually bought out their doomed plant. But that solution is not readily applicable at other failing mills. Although the industry's distress cries for other management-labor accommodations, the suspicions and distrust of decades of hostility are not easily overcome.

What kind of future looms for this failing basic industry? And what hope is there for those thousands of workers displaced as American steel capacity continues to shrink? What are the implications for America's strength? For its defense? For its growth?

How the steel industry achieved greatness is easily understood. How it failed to adapt to changing times is far more complex. Sharp differences exist over remedies to save the industry and, indeed, some knowledgeable experts sincerely doubt it is worth saving.

All the direct quotations in this book come from my personal interviews with the participants in the drama—unless otherwise indicated. I have tried to report all sides. Where the participants perceive events differently, readers must draw their own conclusions. If in passing on this burden I have failed as a historian, I am satisfied I have not failed a duty to history.

CRISIS IN BETHLEHEM

Chapter 1

A VIOLENT BEGINNING

Just how basic a basic industry is was brought home to me one May morning in 1929. I was five years old and neighbors had a few moments before cut down my father's body from a limb of a cherry tree in the backyard of our home in Kingston, Pennsylvania. A Lithuanian immigrant, my father had brought his family to this northeastern Pennsylvania coal region town where he could work the mines.

But the mines fell a victim to the Depression, and, at age thirty-nine, my father fell along with them, defeated in spirit and weakened in body by the coal damage to his lungs. His sole hope, my distraught mother told her children, was that his $200 insurance policy would enable us to join relatives who had settled near Bethlehem, where lay the mecca of Bethlehem Steel, fulfiller of a need so basic that it would forever provide employment to those fortunate enough to be hired.

The relatives who took us in were, alas, not much more

fortunate than we, but from their wooden porch we were at least in sight of steel country. At night we could even see the horizon light up as flames shot into the sky from the blast furnaces at the Bethlehem plant some twenty miles away.

For us, and for thousands of others, those flames meant the hope of a paycheck. When my mother's new husband moved us closer to the city, I learned how a job at "the Steel" was highly coveted even though, for the men, it often meant brutal working conditions. If a daughter was taken on in the office, the family was indeed well blessed.

My brother landed a job in the Bethlehem steel plant as soon as he became of age. I was considered less lucky. I was hired by the city's daily newspaper after high school, and early in 1941 became a night reporter on the draft-depleted news staff of the Bethlehem *Globe-Times*.

To a newcomer, Bethlehem had all the characteristics of smokestack America. Clouds of smoke puffed incessantly from the five-mile-long complex of blast furnaces, open hearths, forges, coke works, and varied mills where twenty-one thousand workers made steel, shaped steel, and shipped steel in forms ranging from five-hundred-ton generator shafts to lightweight building angles you could lift with a finger.

But in a short time, I discovered it was the people in this city of seventy thousand that gave it character. Settled in 1741 by the Moravians, a peace-loving Christian sect, Bethlehem originally was a tight, church-controlled community. Then, during the industrial revolution, waves of immigrants poured in when iron foundries were built and the Lehigh Valley Railroad linked the coal regions to the north and west with metropolitan markets in New York and Philadelphia.

Many evidences of this legacy can be seen in Bethlehem. A handsome complex of preserved and restored buildings from the early Moravian settlement has become the town centerpiece. The impressive campus of Lehigh University, meanwhile, is a living tribute to Asa Packer, the Lehigh Valley Railroad pioneer who founded the school.

The middle Europeans who came to work in the mills

added their own special touches—as you discover by visiting the row homes of their descendants. Many stalwart house-wives still sweep their sidewalks early in the morning. And nearly all the backyards contain a plot of black, mulched soil. In summer each yard overflows with flowers and vegetables, and is often bordered with an arbor of trained grapevines under which a family can sit in the shade.

The dull red dust that escaped from fired-up open hearths was nearly always evident on the windowsills, but was not as repulsive as a visitor might imagine. When I first came to town, the depth of the dust on the window ledges used to be an indication of how much steel the mills were producing, and how much overtime the men were earning. Old-timers insist they could tell from a glance how fat or lean the next pay-checks were likely to be.

As the home office of Bethlehem Steel, the city always had a generous mix of white-collar workers. The steel company attracted people who gladly supported the Bach Choir, who restored and lived in regal old Germanic homes built by the founding Moravians, and who patronized the steady fare of cultural and athletic events at Lehigh University and Mora-vian College, both located within the city.

There also was an opulence about the Saucon Valley Country Club, the lush, steel-subsidized sanctuary that grew to fifty-four championship holes of golf, plus a six-hole prac-tice course, and enabled steel executives to reserve secluded villas well removed from the central clubhouse for private drinking and dancing. Naturally, there was plenty of town gossip about these activities, and never a shortage of people seeking the right introductions to break in.

But Bethlehem was also a scarred city in 1941. The indus-try that had changed it from a quiet, church-owned commu-nity into an important manufacturing center was caught in the turmoil of labor unrest. Bethlehem Steel had become a major target of the union movement that began organizing basic industries after the National Labor Relations Act was passed in 1937.

The union's efforts to gain a foothold at Bethlehem Steel began on June 12, 1936, when twelve trade unionists met in Pittsburgh and founded the Steel Workers Organizing Committee (SWOC). Philip Murray, on loan from the United Mine Workers of America (UMW), was chairman of the committee. Its announced goal was to unionize all steelworkers. At first, many assumed the effort would go the way of previous futile efforts, notably the violent, unsuccessful steel strike at the Homestead Mill of the Carnegie plant in 1892 and the general steel strike of 1919, which ended in bitter defeat for the workers. Those setbacks had established the steel industry as the citadel of business resistance to unionism.

However, two new elements were present now: the clout of John L. Lewis, boss of the United Mine Workers, who assigned top aides and advanced organizing funds from the UMW treasury to help the steelworker organizing effort; and the growing presence of the fledgling Congress of Industrial Organizations (CIO), which recruited some 150 organizers from its various unions and sent them out to conquer steel.

Much of the nation was surprised when the Carnegie-Illinois Steel Corporation, the No. 1 producer that became United States Steel, met with Lewis and signed a contract without even a day's strike in March 1937. However, "Little Steel," which included all other steel companies and then represented about a quarter of the nation's steel production, vowed to resist. For one, Tom M. Girdler, chairman of Republic Steel, announced that he would resign and grow apples before signing with the union.

Republic stockpiled great quantities of pistols, rifles, and tear gas to prepare for a showdown, according to the LaFollette congressional investigating committee. An inevitably bitter strike broke out on May 12, 1937. It reached a bloody climax outside the Republic Steel Plant in Chicago, in what union historians refer to as the "Memorial Day Massacre." Police fired on a parade of strikers and supporters, killing ten and wounding ninety others. The plant managed to keep operating, but the bloodshed did not slow the union tide.

If the unionists were going to be beaten back, Bethlehem Steel, the biggest member of "Little Steel," was seen as the company most likely to do it. Its home office and most of its plants were geographically well away from the agitators stirring the masses in the big cities. Bethlehem was also one of the more benevolent companies. An internal union, known as the Employees Representation Plan (ERP), had been in place for nineteen years, and Bethlehem had led the way in the industry with a company-financed pension plan for blue-collar workers.

However, Bethlehem's biggest protection against outside organizers was its ethnic workers, who valued their jobs and feared to offend their employer. They were not inclined to do anything that might endanger their chances of a better life.

Michael Skertic, now seventy-eight, his wiry body bent over from years of hard labor, was one of Bethlehem's fiercest unionists in that era. He became president of Star Lodge, the first American Federation of Labor (AFL) chapter organized at Bethlehem Steel, thinking every worker with a gripe against the company would flock to sign up after the National Labor Relations Act was passed. He found out how badly he had miscalculated when he tried to pass out union literature to Bethlehem steelworkers.

"They'd see me coming at the gates and would duck inside the plant," he says. "They were afraid to be seen talking to me. They were afraid of getting discriminated against. Afraid of getting a dirtier job. Afraid of ending up with no job."

About the only ones who showed an interest in signing up, Skertic says, were those steelworkers in the dirtiest and most dangerous jobs. Many of these were Mexicans and Portuguese working as chippers, the laborers who chipped defects from steel billets.

"They worked with an air-driven chisel," Skertic explains. "You moved it back and forth on the billet. If you didn't hold the chisel firmly in place, it would fly off. Some workers got hit in the back. Some got hit in the leg. You had no idea when a chisel would come flying off a billet."

The pounding chisels generated dust particles that kept the chipping room in a constant haze, and respirators were unknown. Skertic continues: "One Spanish guy came in from the chipping mill. He had cancer or TB and told me the company was taking away his health benefits, ten bucks a month or whatever. I wrote to the health department in Harrisburg and got him a hearing. I showed up and dumped twenty-five pounds of chips, crust, and dust that the guys had collected for me at the foundry. 'This is what he was breathing,' I said."

The company decided to keep the ex-chipper on health benefits until he died, which was not long after. Skertic's intervention was much appreciated by the rank and file, he says, but it had no noticeable effect on influencing them to join his union.

Discouraged, Skertic went to the AFL convention to plead for organizing help. When the financial report read from the floor disclosed that the union had only $18,000 in the entire international treasury for organizing, Skertic returned home even more dispirited and remained that way, he says, until help came from John L. Lewis and the CIO. He gladly abdicated his AFL base to join the better-heeled CIO.

Joseph Mangan, sixty-eight, a slight, peppery, leather-faced survivor of the union organizing days who became a union local president and a city councilman, started work at Bethlehem Steel in the coke works, a hellishly hot place where the air was dirty, the noise ear-shattering, and a misstep on a hot coke oven could be fatal. He remembers that his first job in the early 1940s was to stand by as a stretcher-bearer while workers "pushed" batteries of coke ovens, which bake coal into the coke that fuels blast furnaces.

"The heat goes up to 190 degrees when they push an oven. A guy wearing wooden shoes walks on the roof to open the oven door. A second guy pushes the coke onto a car, another guy catches it. They push thirty, forty, maybe fifty ovens . . . they push until they keel over. That's where the stretcher-bearers come in."

The hardship of those almost unbearable working conditions was compounded for many workers by the knowledge they would never advance to a better position. "Someone came up with the idea that Hispanics could stand the heat better," Mangan recalls. "Once assigned to the coke oven, that's where they stayed."

Mangan says he became a union activist when he found that newer employees who were white were being assigned to safer and cleaner jobs in the coking operations, bypassing such veteran pushers as Gil Lopez, a respected member of Bethlehem's Mexican community. When Mangan asked the foreman whether seniority counted, he was told all job assignments were at the supervisor's discretion.

Mangan persisted with the foreman, and his intervention did lift Gil Lopez, whose son later became a Bethlehem school principal, up from a hellhole and into a cleaner job at the coke works, but it was only because of Mangan's powers of persuasion. Seniority had no standing as company policy. In fact, favoritism in job assignments at Bethlehem Steel was an open scandal tolerated by the company.

"Jobs were distributed ethnically," Mangan says. The formula and presumed justification went roughly as follows: the Germans (smart) became the machinists. Hungarians (tough) were sent to jobs at the blast furnace. Slovaks (diligent and religious) went to the small mills where Slovak was spoken. The Irish (gutsy but lazy) generally got jobs with the plant patrol. The Mexicans, Portuguese, and other Hispanics (boat jumpers) were put to work where it was hottest and dirtiest.

John Wadolny, a spry, angular veteran of forty-six years in the steel business, reinforces Mangan's recollections.

"At the Bethlehem Steel entrance off Emery Street, there were about twenty small wooden lockers reserved for foremen. The men who worked under them would come to work with eggs, chickens, half a hog, and so on and place them in their boss's [lockers]. It was expected at the time. If a guy wanted a better job, he was told to take care of his boss. And he did.

"But the one thing that turned me strongly toward the

union didn't happen at the plant. It happened outside. Now remember, I'm eighteen. I come from a good Catholic family. I'm working in a section with a bunch of guys mostly in their thirties. I was invited to a party at the Holy Ghost Club where they had bowling. What I saw turned my stomach.

"Two or three of the foremen were there. They were getting all their drinks free. The steelworkers' wives were there too, several of them really beautiful girls. The foremen would feel them up, right in front of their husbands. You know, fondle their breasts and everything. No one would say a thing. I thought to myself: 'Is this the goddamn way you have to get ahead in the steel company?' "

John Posivak, tall, erect, and ruddy, is seventy years old and a master tradesman. He does all the plumbing, carpentry, and even wiring at his neat double-story brick home in one of Bethlehem's middle-class neighborhoods. He risked his job for the union way back in the 1930s, he says, because he was making only 41 cents an hour working ten hours a day in the billet yard. He was attracted by John L. Lewis's call for $5 a day and forty hours a week for all steelworkers.

"I started with SWOC in 1936," Posivak says. "We set out to eliminate the company union. It was rough. [Bethlehem] had pushed us around before, and [now] they made it tougher. We couldn't complain to anyone because we didn't have a friend on the upper levels. What saved me was I caddied for a lot of the golfing bosses at Saucon Valley."

The sons of immigrants—the likes of the Skertics, the Mangans, the Wadolnys and the Posivaks—sought to change the workplace injustices that their parents had learned to accept. For years, they were the ones who passed the union word, urged and at times coerced workers to sign a union card, and risked jobs and promotions to achieve the organizing goals. However, the unionization drive did not succeed until the national political climate changed.

In 1940, the National Labor Relations Board (NLRB), a key agency established under the New Deal, ordered Bethlehem Steel to decertify its Employee Representation Plan. The

NLRB ruled, in effect, that the ERP was an arm of the company and not a bona fide union. The steel workers organizing committee immediately asked that the company enter negotiations toward an NLRB election to select a collective bargaining agent.

The company declared it would appeal the ruling. The steelworkers insisted on immediate recognition. "We had four thousand workers signed up in the plant by now," Posivak says. "But the company wouldn't recognize us with a card check so we told them we would strike." Six months later, on March 24, 1941, after their repeated threats to shut down the plant had been ignored, the steelworkers struck.

During the next four days, I was appalled at the hatred that exploded in Bethlehem. I also became ashamed of the *Globe-Times,* the newspaper that I would someday run as editor. As ugly as the demonstrations were and as much a newcomer as I was to the business, I could sense serious inequities in coverage, and was soon convinced that the newspaper had become a willing company partner in a conspiracy to undermine the strikers.

At the behest of Bethlehem Steel, the city sent police in cruisers to protect nonstrikers trying to enter the gates. The cars were pelted with bricks and stones. Police responded by firing tear gas into the crowd. A police car was overturned, and several officers were taken to the hospital.

The *Globe-Times* nonetheless featured a company statement on page one that day, proclaiming that all men were working. A companion story ominiously pointed out that the strikers were jeopardizing $1 billion in defense contracts at Bethlehem Steel.

Pennsylvania Governor Arthur H. James ordered all state liquor stores closed, and the police shut down taprooms in steel neighborhoods. The Northampton County sheriff notified the governor that he could not control the situation with the men at his disposal and asked for state police reinforcements.

"Riding high on prancing horses and swinging skull-cracking riot sticks with abandon, a squad of state motor police started breaking up pickets at the Main Gate," read the next day's lead story in the *Globe-Times*. The paper now featured a company statement saying that the plant was running with 80 percent of the men on the job. A sidebar story quoted Rep. Martin Dies, chairman of the House Un-American Activities Committee, as saying he had evidence that the steelworkers organizing committee was communist-infiltrated and that the strike was a conspiracy to halt the war effort.

Violence escalated as angry mobs overturned an estimated two hundred cars, mostly owned by nonstriking workers trying to cross the picket lines, and dumped many of the vehicles into the Lehigh River. Yet the newspaper continued to report that company operations were virtually unaffected.

A federal mediator, meeting with both sides throughout the night, settled the strike on March 28, 1941. An NLRB election was held at Bethlehem Steel in August, and SWOC, which shortly afterward became the United Steelworkers of America, CIO, was handily certified.

Bethlehem, the last major steel producer to resist, had succumbed to the organizers. Such was the humble and violent beginning of a union that would go on to win the highest manufacturing wages in the country and become labor's pacesetter for basic industry.

Chapter 2

THE COMFORTS
OF INSULARITY

Agood way to begin understanding the distress of the steel industry is to visit the Moravian Church's ancient Nisky Hill Cemetery in Bethlehem. Here, on a bluff overlooking the enormous Bethlehem Steel plant beside the Lehigh River, are buried many of the leaders of the corporation. You can often guess the rank of the interred by the size of the gravestone.

Dominating over all his colleagues in death, as he did in life, is Eugene G. Grace, who with founder Charles Schwab built Bethlehem Steel into the nation's No. 2 steel producer. A huge open rotunda marks Grace's grave. A semicircular granite bench capable of seating twenty people has been provided for any who might come to pay homage to the departed chairman.

Next to Grace lie the remains of William H. Johnstone, a farsighted man who became head of Bethlehem's powerful finance committee in steel's bonanza years and was one of the few in the top echelon to challenge Grace's fundamental strategy. Johnstone, who had moved to New York City in retirement, returned to Bethlehem to die, virtually unnoticed. He lies, at his own request, under a simple flat granite slab.

The markers are valid symbols of the differing philosophies that competed at Bethlehem—one that bred the current crisis and one that might have enabled the company to prevent it.

Grace stressed the need for Bethlehem Steel to keep expanding its capacity. "I have no doubt that the story will be one of increasing per capita use of steel in spite of the development of competing materials," Grace declared in the mid-1950s, in one of his last official statements. "I have no qualms about excess capacity. The United States will never catch up to its material needs and aspirations."

Grace's philosophy, even many years after he died, senile at age eighty-three, in 1960, greatly influenced his successors at Bethlehem Steel. The chief executives of the other big steel producers by and large agreed with this strategy. Steel, they assured themselves, could be expected to thrive as long as they could expand capacity.

While never demeaning Grace's remarkable achievements during fifty years in Bethlehem, Johnstone was one of the few steel executives, as far back as the 1950s, who saw the future differently. When the reins of finance fell into his grip after Grace's death, Johnstone spoke of new forces in the economy, of revolutionary new technology to replace old steelmaking practices, and of traditional markets giving way to international competition. He could foresee a changing world and knew that Bethlehem Steel had to change with it.

But while the world did change, much as Johnstone predicted, Bethlehem Steel did not. Nor did the other major steel producers, until engulfed by a tide they could not hold back. "Steel is America," John Gunther, the best-selling author of the postwar era, wrote in *Inside U.S.A.* It was a truism, in the minds of steel executives and the public alike, that steel would be forever basic and therefore forever profitable.

When I became editor of the Bethlehem *Globe-Times* in

1956, the steel industry was at high tide. Bethlehem made $161,411,625 that year and profits rose to more than $191,-000,000 in 1957. The signs of prosperity were often embarrassingly conspicuous. In 1959, for example, the *Globe-Times* republished *Business Week*'s listings of the highest paid executives for the previous year.

Bethlehem Steel had seven names in the top ten, starting with Arthur B. Homer, chairman, the highest-paid corporate officer in the United States. His salary and bonuses totaled $511,249, which translated into today's dollars would be equivalent to about $1,900,000. Still, for a steel chairman in those times that was only a mediocre year. In 1957, the big year before, Homer had received $623,336, which would have put his annual compensation well above $2,000,000 in today's dollars.

One would expect such hefty salaries and bonuses to be rewards for entrepreneurship, or at least for visionary management. Far from it. This corporate elite was so well-compensated merely because American steel companies had an unchallenged grip on the marketplace.

From the end of World War II into the late 1950s, American steel mills could sell all they produced at almost any price. They enjoyed what economists call an oligopoly, where a few big firms control the market—and the profits. When steelworkers struck or threatened to strike at the expiration of a contract, the companies, which were all bound by the same industry-wide labor agreement, handed out wage increases and benefits that outran all others in U.S. industry. Then the big steel firms raised prices to whatever levels were necessary to satisfy profits, stockholder returns, and the new pay scales.

Donald Swan, a member of the Bethlehem Steel legal staff who left to become a vice president at Jones and Laughlin Steel and now runs an investment consulting office, recalls the mood: "Bethlehem at that time had the reputation that its hallways were lined with gold, and when you became employed there they gave you a pick to mine [it]."

Paul Marshall, a former Harvard Business School professor who became a consultant to steel companies, has a sterner view of that period. "I think the steel industry was mismanaged in the sense that they were insensitive to anything but their own internal activities," he says.

Bethlehem Steel is a perfect example of how a company lulled itself into a parochial view of the world. Eugene Grace wanted corporate uniformity. He not only created an inbred board consisting only of officers employed within the company, but also established the precedent for board behavior: lunch together in the corporate dining room, golf together in the afternoon, socializing together in the evening. His word was law. It prevailed in all decisions from building new open hearths to installing a new sand trap on the tenth hole of the Saucon Valley Country Club's old course.

At lunch time, for instance, administrative personnel at Bethlehem Steel's headquarters building on Third Street were segregated in separate dining areas. The board gathered in the largest and most elegant room, and members took their fixed places around the table, occupying identical leather chairs, each with the name of its occupant affixed to it on a chromium-plated badge. A spacious, paneled dining room was reserved daily for the sales department. The six smaller private dining rooms off the fifth-floor corridor served each department under a vice president. Entrance by invitation only was the rule, and also in the main dining room, where separate tables were reserved for separate departments. Only the cafeteria was open to anyone.

Many bright, middle-management executives found the environment suffocating. Obligated to work and relax solely with assigned company members, they were dismayed by their lack of access to the real decision-makers.

Undoubtedly there were advantages to a tightly knit board, but Bethlehem's top executives were so removed from the real world that they rarely encountered a fresh point of view. Living close to their offices, they rode no commuter express where a fertile-minded outsider might ask, "What's the matter with you guys at Bethlehem? Haven't you caught on to what's happening in the rest of the world?"

In my first eight years as editor of the *Globe-Times,* I rarely saw a top Bethlehem Steel executive in the community. One of the few times I saw a major steel executive outside his working environment was when Joseph Larkin, a vice president whose $467,082 in earnings put him in the nation's top ten in 1958, called on my publisher, Rolland L. Adams, to protest an editorial I had written questioning the latest steel price increase. When Larkin lodged his objections with me directly, I was appalled that a person drawing that kind of money could only argue—"Bethlehem Steel is very important to this town"—suggesting therefore that the company should be above criticism.

If Bethlehem Steel was insensitive to the world outside, it certainly was well aware of the world's finest creature comforts. In fact, it created a department of General Services to enhance the good life. This department took care of the perquisites for the deserving within the company.

The story of General Services is the story of the Bethlehem Steel career of Frank Rabold, a strapping ex-wrestler and Lehigh University football player.

Just before his graduation from Lehigh in 1939, Rabold received an invitation from the personnel manager at Bethlehem Steel to join the "loop course," the company's management training program. He accepted, and within a few short years became one of the company's most influential managers, his rise to eminence coming without his making or selling a single bar of steel.

When Bethlehem's top executives decided to make the Saucon Valley Country Club, already famous for its championship golf course, into even more of a showplace, Rabold took on his first major assignment. He was given an open pocketbook to hire the top consultants in the country and produced the appropriate results. Stunning chandeliers, among other interior touches, soon brightened the decor of the staid country club building. A magnolia terrace connected a new three-pool swimming complex with the club's indoor-outdoor lounge. Squash courts and indoor tennis courts were installed within new, architecturally compatible buildings. Even the bridge crossing little Saucon Creek was a showpiece, built for an estimated $100,000 in 1950 dollars. Bethlehem Steel paid all the big bills, sparing members the capital assessments that normal country clubs would impose.

Meanwhile, the company's plant supervisors were not forgotten. In the late 1940s, Chairman Grace tried to head off attempts to unionize the supervisors (which would have been legal in those pre-Taft-Hartley Act days) by creating some goodwill. An avid (and excellent) golfer himself, Grace could see that building the plant managers their own country club would be a form of good labor relations.

Bethlehem Steel built the supervisors a challenging eighteen-hole golf course, later adding clubhouse, pool, and tennis on a site of wooded hillsides and pleasant meadows. The company named the facility "The Bethlehem Steel Club" and members eligible because of their work status at the plant could join for dues that started at $20 a year. And when complaints of "what about us?" were heard from the rank and file, Bethlehem Steel donated the money for a land swap and underwrote the professional expertise that enabled the city of Bethlehem, during the 1950s, to build a first-class eighteen-hole public golf course that could be used by any resident.

Grace's successors at Bethlehem Steel maintained the company's devotion to the sport well after he departed. During the golf boom of the 1960s, complaints began to be heard that so many people were now playing golf that officers with important guests sometimes had to wait to tee off at Saucon Valley. Concerns were voiced that Saucon's thirty-six-hole layout (not counting the six practice holes) was becoming inadequate.

The argument for adding a new facility gained strength when President Stewart Cort, who later served as chairman between 1970 and 1974, came out to the parking lot after a morning of golf and found a young mother dressed in golf clothes changing her baby's diaper on the hood of his car. A new eighteen-hole championship golf course with limited admission—and absolutely no women allowed—soon was built at company expense on a former steel executive's estate nearby. Henceforth, important guests could tee off at Weyhill, Bethlehem Steel's really exclusive golf club. While the ban against women at Weyhill was partially lifted later to permit them Sunday afternoon play, the course remains one of the most exclusive in the East. At a White House reception for the American Society of Newspaper Editors in 1975, President Ford spotted my name badge, gripped my hand, and exclaimed, "Bethlehem! What a golf course."

A standing function of Rabold's crews was to make sure not only that the golf courses were appropriately groomed, but also that the homes of the company's top executives were adequately maintained and secure.

There were perks to be enjoyed, too, from the company's fleet of seven airplanes, also supervised by Rabold. They were intended for business use, but business was sometimes loosely defined—at least until a vice president was hit with a substantial bill from the Internal Revenue Service for using a company plane to transport his children to college and for weekend trips to an upstate New York hideaway.

Airplane rules required rather specific logs. It was easier to escape IRS surveillance by using Bethlehem Steel's chauffeur service, which General Services also provided. Cars and chauffeurs were assigned at call to those at vice presidential level and above. It was routine for wives to accompany husbands to New York and place the car on standby while they shopped or went to the theater.

Rabold discusses these company policies with no apologies, but insists on making two things clear: executives were assessed for yard work and service calls to their homes at better than going rates, and what is morality today was not morality in those days. "I can remember so many things that no one used to consider improper but today—boom!" he says.

Neither were General Service functions solely self-serving. Many communities and institutions where Bethlehem Steel plants are located benefited from expensive engineering, traffic, and urban renewal studies made by recognized consultants hired by Rabold's department. In the city of Bethlehem, the New York firm of Clarke and Rapuano did the studies that form the basis of center city planning, redevelopment, and an expressway link to an interstate highway. Bethlehem Steel paid the bill.

Of the private institutions that benefited from Bethlehem Steel's largesse, none fared better than neighboring Lehigh University, one of the country's leading engineering schools. As Eugene Grace's alma mater, it had long had close ties with the steel company. When Rabold became a Lehigh trustee and headed its buildings and grounds committee, the company permitted him to assign two men and a secretary, all on the General Services payroll, primarily to university work.

However, nothing symbolized the company's extravagance more than the new office building it erected on an open cornfield on the northern side of the Lehigh River, well removed from the steel plant. To the surprise of virtually no one, the building had direct access to the expressway link that Bethlehem Steel had earlier helped finance for the city. The $35-million, twenty-one-story structure was built in the shape of a cruciform, instead of the traditional rectangle that most designers would say is more functional and economical.

The experts in his office of design and construction were well aware of the added expense, Rabold says, but felt their choice best accommodated the desires of the top executives at Bethlehem. "Their positions were reflected by the location of their offices in the building," he explains. "The vice presidents were in the corners. They had [to have] windows in two directions so it was out of that desire that we came up with the design of a cruciform."

Shortly after the contract was let in 1972, the office of

design and construction was eliminated, and so was most of Rabold's empire, which by now had twelve different departments employing two thousand workers, all earning steelworker wages or above. However, the breakup was not because of corporate conscience-searching on wasteful spending.

The department was done in by the surreptitious actions of a single employee, one Henry Boileau, a suave and fast-stepping manager whom Rabold had put in charge of municipal affairs. Boileau had the authority to let out contracts up to $10,000 without prior approval. He was charged with writing many of them to himself via phony business fronts that he used to bill Bethlehem for services never performed or supplies never delivered.

The bilking grew to $780,000 (or as a steel spokesman put it, "$780,000 of unproductive projects") but no one at Bethlehem Steel noticed anything awry until the Internal Revenue acted. Only when the IRS slapped a hefty lien on Boileau for taxes on unreported income did it dawn on anyone at the company that it had been had.

Rabold, who had been blameless in the defalcations, never regained his old authority and retired in 1980 at age sixty-two.

William Humphries, Rabold's subordinate who signed the Boileau invoices in all innocence, lost his job soon afterward and later sadly reflected on the episode. "Fran Murray [a steel accountant] said to me once, 'You know, it seems to me that Henry Boileau is spending an awful lot of money.' And I said, 'Yes, it does seem like a lot.' That's the way things were checked at Bethlehem Steel."

The saga of General Services is, of course, a blip on the books of a company that had become used to annual profits exceeding a hundred million dollars. But it points up the priorities that had become important at Bethlehem Steel, at a time when its leaders should have been anticipating dramatic changes in their industry.

Chapter 3

A TEST OF MANHOOD

"We had one fellow who was blown into the ladle as we tapped a heat of steel.

"You would think that the human body would melt immediately, you know, the steel is bubbling at about twenty-nine hundred degrees Fahrenheit. But frankly things don't melt that easily. They told me that the heels and the safety helmet floated for some time afterward."

—A steelworker on conditions in the 1950s

AT a time when steel industry tycoons were dominating the compensation rankings in U.S. industry and business, the American blue-collar steelworkers were pushing out record tons of steel—and bitching over the inequities. The contrast between the high life in corporate offices and the often intolerable working conditions in the bowels of the plants during the post–World War II years has left a deeply rooted source of hostility among the rank and file. Those fissures complicate the steel industry's problems even today.

In spite of all the advances in technology and safety, the rigors of steelmaking still feed the unions' suspicion that the company profits extravagantly by exploiting workers and then casting them aside after their muscles have been spent or their lungs exhausted—assuming they have survived the daily perils of their work.

The legendary story of a steelworker's disappearance into a vat of boiling steel is told in every big steel mill. As an editor in the home city of Bethlehem Steel, I can testify that it is more than legend. Newspaper files bulge with articles reporting accidental death or injuries in the mill by crushing, gassing, and, yes, even extinction in hot metal.

Steelmaking is dangerous. It is also tough, dirty, and repetitive. Why then did so many men more than willingly endure the hardships? Obviously, waves of immigrants saw a job at the mill as a foothold in America. And eventually the industry paid high wages. However, after years of living with steelworkers and listening to them talk about their jobs, I am convinced the appeal of the work was more than money. The men were drawn to the mills because steelmaking is a rugged test of manhood and virility.

Steelworkers believe that their skills set them above anyone else in manufacturing and that they have the most demanding jobs in industrial America. Anyone who has the muscle can swing a pick and mine coal, they will tell you. Robots can assemble automobiles. But it takes uncommon talent, a strong body, and a mind that knows no fear to be able to transform piles of red dirt and scrap into the molten metal that is poured, rolled, and pounded into the various shapes that support the mainframes of civilization.

The artistry of making steel starts with iron ore, the basic ingredient in steel. Iron ore is not a rare mineral—it is estimated that 5 percent of the earth's crust is composed of iron. Before the turn of the century, timber cutters in Minnesota accidentally helped locate one of the richest iron ore veins in the world simply by informing mining interests about the rich, red soil in the cavity of an overturned tree. This led to the development of the famous Mesabi range, where ore was so close to the surface it could be shoveled out of pits. However, finding ore in concentrated form usually challenges metallurgical scientists. Today, geologists flying in small airplanes at low altitudes use aeromagnetic surveys to locate deposits thousands of feet beneath the surface, not only in the United States but in many primitive parts of the world.

In Bethlehem, as in most northern steelmaking cities, you could tell winter was near by the buildup of the ore yards. They would overflow by November in the annual race to pile up a safe inventory before the Great Lakes froze for the season.

Iron ore feeds the blast furnaces, those one-hundred-foot-high convoluted structures that look like smoke-stained dinosaurs snorting into the sky. The ore is mixed with other materials from a variety of sources. Steelmakers say a ton of steel may require iron ore shipped from Minnesota, limestone from Ohio, coke from coal mined in West Virginia, manganese ore from Brazil, and scrap from almost any junkyard in the nation.

A tremendous volume of preheated air is blown into the blast furnace in order to start reducing iron ore into liquid iron. The hot air fires the coke, the coal residue, which then becomes incandescent. As the ore melts, a steady stream of hot metal drops to the bottom of the furnace, where it accumulates. The jetlike noise in the smelting process becomes so deafening that conversation becomes impossible.

"The most dangerous part of the blast furnace is the carbon monoxide," says George Kotich, a hard-driving foreman who retired in 1984 after forty years in the Bethlehem plant. "You can't smell it. In the old days when you got gassed, they used to walk you along the Lehigh River for fresh air. Now they put you in a blanket and call the ambulance. And today they have these gas alarms everywhere, even in the elevator."

The blast furnace produces iron without extracting all of the impurities. The hot metal drains into a submarinelike railroad car stationed next to the furnace. In the traditional process that prevailed during the bonanza years, it then goes to the open hearth for refining. Even after the blast furnace has been drained of its molten iron—the so-called "cast,"— the perils remain for the workers. Kotich says he will never forget what happened after a cast was completed at Blast

Furnace D one day in March of 1948. "Seven dead, and I was there," he says. "They put too much water in the furnace to flush it out. The furnace was down but the stock was hot. When the water hit, the place blew up."

Every steelworker soon learns that water is an enemy whenever hot metal is around. The expansion of steam or water is one of the most violent forms of energy.

The next step is to refine the iron into steel. While the process changes, the dangers don't diminish. The open hearth is a rectangular furnace of refractory brickwork built within a heavy steel frame. This was where steel was made during the industry's glory years. Now, just as the open hearths replaced the once-revolutionary Bessemer furnaces as the most popular method of steelmaking, they have in turn been replaced by more efficient basic oxygen furnaces. Yet open hearth furnaces made 90 percent of the ingots produced in this country as recently as the 1950s, and they are still used today at even such major facilities as Bethlehem Steel's Sparrow Point plant in Maryland, Inland Steel in south Chicago, and U.S. Steel's Fairless Works in eastern Pennsylvania.

In sharp contrast to the blast furnace, the open hearth uses an oxidizing process. A typical "charge" contains 50 percent hot iron from the blast furnace, 49 percent scrap, and small amounts of limestone and iron ore. About 40 percent of the energy required to melt and refine a batch of steel, commonly called a heat, comes from the temperatures of the already hot metal and the heat-producing reactions involving oxygen and the impurities in the charge. The other 60 percent of the energy comes from fuel, usually coke oven gas, natural gas, or oil injected into the furnace by water-cooled burners.

Turning out a high-quality order of steel depends on the intuition and skill of men making spot judgments while they are literally under fire. That is why the blue-collar elite were picked to man the open hearths.

Open hearth crews are coordinated by a melter foreman, ideally a mentally tough leader with the combined talents of platoon sergeant, band leader, and master chef, who supervises five open hearths. The first helper, directly under him, commands the highest hourly pay in the shop and sometimes earns more than his foreman. He is responsible for the charging, refining, maintenance, and control of his furnace. Assisting him is the second helper, whose main job is to obtain all the alloys for the heat in progress and to tap the heat when it is ready to go. Physical strength is a must in this job. It is not uncommon for the second helper to have to lift and move five hundred pounds of a manganese alloy with a wheelbarrow. Each group of furnaces has three or four third helpers who are also expected to have brawn. They assist the second helper when the tapping begins and must swing a sledgehammer or brave the heat where directed. They also work with the first helper on routine furnace maintenance.

The furnace men wear long underwear the year around: in summer to protect them against the heat and in winter to protect them against the cold. In summer, temperatures around the furnace exceed 140 degrees and a touch of the railing will raise a blister. Since the buildings are drafty structures with open ends and sidings to provide for the rapid escape of smoke, fumes, and dust, it's not unusual during the winter to see snow on the floor no more than ten feet away from the furnaces.

Overhead cranes carry ladles of hot metal processed at the blast furnace and pour the metal into the open hearth. As soon as the liquid iron, which is still about 2500 degrees and very active, contacts the inert, partially melted materials, the furnace starts boiling violently. Looking into the interior of an open hearth at this stage is like looking down the throat of an active volcano. Huge globs of metal, fist-size and sometimes larger, begin to leap above the surface. For the next five hours, the standard length of time for a refining cycle, the furnace crews swing into a synchronized ritual that many in the industry say is an art form.

The first helper puts on cobalt-blue glasses and assesses the wild reactions inside the hearth by peering through a peephole in one of the water-cooled furnace doors. Great volumes of water are used to cool every critical part of the furnace. That explains why steel mills are built along rivers or lake fronts. The first helper appraises both the temperature and composition of the liquid bath. From time to time, he extracts samples of slag and steel with a long-handled spoon and pours the molten steel on the ground to check its fluidity and approximate composition.

Meanwhile, the melter foreman makes his own visual checks of the five furnaces under his supervision. If he has reason to challenge a first helper's appraisal, the foreman will poke a bar of steel into the furnace. He watches to see whether it comes out with a straight cut or "like a rat's tail." He even monitors the size of the bubbles before making a judgment on how the charge is progressing.

If the charge appears to be melted, the first helper makes certain by probing all areas of the hearth's bottom with a long one-inch-square bar affectionately termed a "Hunky periscope." The first samples are sent to the lab for tests to determine whether the batch of steel meets a customer's specifications. If the results show the carbon content to be too high, for example, more iron ore is added. If carbon is too low, hot metal from the blast furnace is added. If the sulfur and/or the phosphorus content is too high, burnt lime is added, and then fluorspar, to accelerate the reduction of these undesirable elements. Finally, if the temperature is too low or high, fuel input is raised or lowered.

The ultimate test of steelmaking stamina occurs on the open hearth floor when more refractory materials must be fed onto the furnace banks. When the door is opened, fierce tongues of flame leap out. Led by the first helper, the furnacemen line up with shovels of materials in hand and one after another move toward the opening. At the last possible instant, with a long and graceful swing, each shovels his load into the furnace, finishing with a follow-through that places arm and shoulder in front of one's face to protect it from the flames. Any shoveler who misses can expect lasting ridicule.

When the melter determines that the heat of steel is ready

to be tapped, he tells the first helper to "wrap up," which is the signal to summon the entire furnace crew to that particular furnace. Each furnace has its own distinctive wrap-up alarm. Some use bells salvaged from scrapped railroad steam engines. Others simply have someone swing a sledgehammer at a suspended disk of steel. The men in the furnace area know by the sound which furnace is ready.

While the first helper extracts the last sample of steel to be sent to the lab, the second helper moves into the searing heat behind the furnace and starts digging out materials solidified in the taphole. When it is partially cleared, he takes a small explosive charge, sticks it into the taphole, and backs away.

The hot steel comes out with such force that second helpers have been knocked down or even into the waiting ladle below. It is a dangerous moment. Until workers were secured with safety belts and protective railings were installed above the ladles, this operation was the scene of many accidents. If anyone falls into a ladle, not even a partial body could be retrieved. I haven't found a news clip to document it, but Paul Buck, a highly respected foreman who retired from Bethlehem in 1984, heard of one worker who slipped and vanished into a ladle of hot steel. When no remnant of the victim could be retrieved, the company reportedly buried the entire ladle at the cinder dump.

The liquid steel is poured into ingot molds that are transported by cars running on narrow gauge rails. Overhead cranes remove molds when the ingots are partially solidified and their centers still liquid at about 2200° F, ingots are then sent to soaking pits where they are reheated and their temperatures homogenized. Once that occurs, the ingots are ready for the primary rolling mills. There, and then in the finishing mills, they are rolled into the shapes desired by the customer.

Dangers lurk in every processing step. Consider the routine perils in a furnace man's typical shift. He can slip from the open hearth platform and fall into the pit below, which is filled with jagged metal stalagmites and hot slag. On the charging floor, he has to avoid the steam engines carrying boiling hot metal back and forth. Overhead, cranes constantly carry loads of scrap, pieces of which inevitably fall from the magnet. And ever present is the possibility of a steel breakout on the floor or an explosion of metal from the furnace bath.

The gruesome accidents that occur in steelmaking are reported, but seldom detailed, in daily newspapers. Limbs are shattered when men are squeezed between moving equipment. Faces are burned and disfigured by hot metal erupting from a furnace. The public reads about the tragedies but does not always learn about the many near-tragedies. Lew Field, a former open hearth supervisor with forty years experience, tells of a furnaceman knocked into the ladle just before the steel rushed out. He could not climb out because the container was fifteen feet deep. An expert craneman lowered his hook just ahead of the torrent of hot steel and kept the incident from becoming a front-page story.

Yet no number of such horror stories ever diminished enthusiasm for working at the open hearth. This is where steelmaking artistry flourished, and where dedication was most rewarded. Fathers encouraged sons to vie for jobs at the furnace. They worked alongside each other, as did uncles, brothers, and cousins. The open hearth, where steel was melted, traditionally became, for those who proved their stamina, the melting pot for ethnic groups—Hungarians, Italians, Germans, Irish, Slavs, and Hispanics. A variety of tongues were spoken and formal introductions were seldom made. The men called one another by such names as "Big Mike," "Little Mike," and "Bulldog Mike;" "Young Martin," "Old Martin," and "Shamrock;" "Black Hand," "Tomahawk," and "Popeye;" "Wild Bill," "Tricky Mickey," and "Snowshoe;" and a slew of "Slims," "Fats," and "Patsys."

This breed of worker gave corporate "fat cats" little respect. In fact, some of the long-time melters refused to identify with either the union or the company, claiming their own role in steelmaking was unique. Those outspoken attitudes seemed to be catching all the way down the line—for entire furnace crews.

Mary Scranton, the wife of former Pennsylvania governor and congressman William Scranton, discovered this independence one day while touring the Bethlehem plant. A visitors' platform had been erected in an open hearth shop especially to accommodate touring parties. Mrs. Scranton was invited to move from the platform to the actual furnace area and detonate the explosive charge that would tap the heat. The second helper setting up the tap was a barrel-chested, tobacco-chewing furnaceman.

"What happens if the charge doesn't go off?" a nervous Mrs. Scranton asked. To which the second helper, between chews of tobacco, replied, "Well, lady, then we're fucked!"

The American steel industry remained wedded to the open hearths during its period of heaviest expansion. By the mid-1960s, it was clear the basic oxygen furnace (BOF) was technologically superior. Open hearths, which require external infusions of a variety of fuels, take six to eight hours to make a batch of steel. The pear-shaped BOFs, which need no external source of fuel and feature supersonic injection of pure oxygen, take forty-five minutes to produce the same batch. However, the industry did not rush to phase out the open hearths. While Bethlehem Steel has a modern BOF shop at its plant at Sparrows Point, Maryland, the seven 420-ton open hearth furnaces installed in 1958—the last to be built in the United States—were still in operation in 1986.

Naturally, steelmaking is much safer today, and it is mandatory to use such basic equipment as safety shoes and glasses, flame retardent clothes and respirators. Educational programs to reduce the human factor in accidents are conducted in all plants, and no piece of new equipment is installed without worker safety-orientation.

The long reign of steelmaking by open hearths must be regarded as a significant era of industrial history. It tells much about the breed of men who made the steel that built the bay-conquering bridges, the metropolitan skyscrapers, and much else of modern America. Knowing of those difficult years makes it easier to understand how organized labor would find little difficulty in rallying rank and file support for work place improvements, and how difficult it is now for the men to give anything back.

Chapter 4

BETHLEHEM STEEL AT HOME

WHILE the workers at Bethlehem Steel endure many hardships on the job, they have one advantage over the executive staff that was not negotiated in any contract. They have no requirement, in their social lives, to demonstrate their compatibility with the corporation.

When the 7-to-3 shift heads for the gates on a Friday afternoon, workers have the option of heading for the bowling alley, home, the bar, or wherever their impulses take them. At just about the same time, the high-salaried official in Bethlehem's main offices is checking his calendar to see which dinner party he and his wife must attend that night. Most likely, he can look forward to the same type of exercise on Saturday night, and he may even have to perform through a weekend golf match followed by clubhouse poker. All the social events will be held within a five-mile radius; all will be attended by the executives he deals with daily on the job.

Thus, the in-house competition that exists among executives, department heads, and their would-be successors continues even after office doors are closed for the night. Unlike members of corporations based in large cities, Bethlehem Steel officials are expected to locate in certain preferred neighborhoods; their homes are never more than a few minutes' driving time from company headquarters. Proximity to the Saucon Valley Country Club is highly approved for leading executives; the road leading to the club has become known as Vice President's Row. Ostensibly, the intent has been to build team spirit.

Conforming to the corporation's mores does not end with the executive. His wife (very few women have achieved executive status at Bethlehem Steel) is all but given a script to follow. Her wardrobe, topics of conversation, general appearance, drinking habits, skills as a hostess, and certainly her devotion to her husband and his career are carefully scrutinized. Her husband's future with the company well may depend upon the impression she makes, especially if her husband is competing for a promotion.

The rules have been relaxed somewhat since the social upheaval of the late 1970s, and the social glue has melted most definitely in recent years, when fiscal distress forced many of the most straight-backed staffers into early retirement. But when Bethlehem Steel was in its ascendancy during the postwar boom years of the fifties and sixties, the social demands on its executives were often as exhaustive as the administrative.

Certain taboos—such as a wife with a personal career— were rarely tolerated. An inclination to the Democratic Party was considered a sign of disloyalty; and if politics was discussed at a dinner party, it was a man's topic and women were expected only to listen.

One executive wife broke the rules at a dinner party at the home of Stewart S. Cort, then president of Bethlehem Steel, shortly after Richard Nixon won the election in 1972.

She became exasperated because Cort, who spent much of his career in Bethlehem Steel's California offices, "was going on and on about how marvelous Nixon had been out there and what a great president he was going to be in the eyes of history.

"I had been following Nixon's career, too, and I knew it wasn't all that good," she says, "and, besides, the arm of every corporate officer at Bethlehem Steel had been twisted to give to the Nixon campaign. I resented Nixon macing my husband, so I foolishly blurted out my feelings.

" 'Well, I voted for McGovern,' I said."

The room felt silent. An angry Cort, his face reddening, leaped from his chair and glared at her.

"You voted for McGovern?" he shouted. "You don't mean it!"

The punishment for her indiscretion did not end there.

"At the next board meeting, Cort took the occasion to tell the directors that I had too big a mouth," she says. "He told them I was talking about politics, which was none of my business, and that someone ought to get the word to my husband to straighten me out. So I never discussed politics again."

Comments from wives indicated that any serious thought was also suspect. This so frustrated some women that they formed a clandestine group that discussed—of all things—good books.

The frustration in some cases had more damaging effects. Alcoholism took its toll on a number of wives, who were sent off to dry-out clinics until they could again take their proper place in the company's social life. Such delinquency was usually tolerated if it did not interfere with the husband's efforts on the job or cause public embarrassment.

The cloistered role for the wives, back in the fifties and sixties, reflected the cultural insecurity of the company's officials, then the highest paid industrial managers in the country. Although most were college graduates, their wives frequently were not. The need to establish social credentials was paramount and role models were eagerly sought. No woman sent tremors through ambitious steel families more than that wife who came to the company with a Seven Sisters' degree, a collection of heirloom silver, and a lineage of old money. This type was home free. She could do as she pleased, join the organizations she chose, and always be accepted at the highest company level.

For the majority of wives, however, such license was an unavailable luxury. For them membership even in the non-partisan League of Women Voters was taboo (although they coveted and sought enrollment in the Junior League). The Ladies' Auxiliary of St. Luke's Hospital, church work, and family duties were the approved ways to use spare time. Later, during the seventies and assuredly in the eighties, opportunities broadened to include working with youth services and health agencies. The right to pursue their own careers also became acceptable.

Lucky was the organization that captured the attention of a steel chairman's wife. A whole retinue of eager volunteers was sure to follow. When Marge Foy, wife of Chairman Lewis Foy who headed the company from 1974 to 1980, plunged into volunteer work with the American Cancer Society, the local chapter became the biggest fund raiser in the state. This was due in large part to the support she received from steel executives' wives.

Bethlehem Steel also clearly defined the role of its male executives. In the 1950s, Ted Martin, a former Baltimore *Sun* newsman hired by Bethlehem as a speech writer, was ordered to resign from the board of the local American Red Cross chapter. If there was to be any diversion of executive talent to outside causes, he was told, the company expected to make those assignments.

For many years, a single community relations employee was assigned to represent the company with those civic organizations, such as the United Fund and Chamber of Commerce, which the corporation chose to support. In local elections, he wrote checks for candidates of both parties, although incumbents got something extra. This sole Bethlehem representative sometimes participated in as many as six functions a day, taking in breakfast meetings, luncheons, cocktail receptions, and banquets. The mortality rate for the job was understandably high until Jim Robertson, a diet-conscious teetotaller, proved it was possible to survive in the post.

Executives and their wives were encouraged to participate in the youth agencies that served steelworkers' sons and daughters. Middle managers clamored to be named to the boards of the Boys' Club and the Boy Scouts because the highest steel officials lent their names and dollars to those causes. However, agencies that dealt with low-income housing, civil rights, or—heaven forbid—nuclear disarmament were too controversial. The community thus was denied considerable volunteer talent in these areas, and the company was prepared to fire any executive, as we shall see, who out of conscience defied the edict.

The results of Bethlehem Steel's lack of involvement in the more controversial aspects of the community were quite evident when I became editor of the *Globe-Times* in the mid-1950s.

A *laissez-faire* relationship existed between the company and the Democratic Party clique that ran City Hall. The south side of the city, where the steel plant and offices were located, was a mecca for bordellos, illegal gambling spas, and filthy tenements.

The steel company was more than willing to tolerate bad government, I soon concluded, because it is easier to control. For example, when the incompetent street commissioner exhausted his budget early, he would come to the company, hat in hand, and ask for tons of slag and crushed stone, which are used for laying down road foundations. Conversely, when the company, or one of its executives, wanted a street repaired or a special snow-clearance given, the debt could be called.

When extraordinary expenses or just sloppy management drained the city budget before taxes were due, the politicians knew the steel company would pay its taxes in advance. In return, when Bethlehem Steel needed zoning exceptions or other municipal favors, it could count on help from the top. In fact, one of my earliest editorial challenges of the city's special treatment of the company occurred when a Bethlehem

Steel-designated contractor was granted an outrageous 110-percent height variance from the zoning laws.

Happily, the city did change for the better and so did Bethlehem Steel's sense of civic responsibility, but not by design. The impetus came from an unlikely source, a city councilman whose uncle, visiting Bethlehem, was victimized in a bordello on Diamond Street, virtually adjoining the steel plant. The uncle's girl for the night stole his wallet containing $800. The councilman, trying to force his way into the house and get the money back, fired several shots from a revolver, rousing an entire neighborhood in the predawn hours. The police tried to cover up the incident, but the *Globe-Times* was able to find enough witnesses to publish the story.

While it could be argued that the councilman's attempt to help a visitor was one of the more selfless acts of his political career, the notoriety aroused our sleepy town. The publicity also awakened Bethlehem Steel to what was happening to the image of its home-office city. The incident gave crucial impetus to the election of a reform government, featuring the first Republican mayor in Bethlehem's history and a new home-rule charter.

For the next two decades, from 1960 to 1980, the city enjoyed a renaissance of modernization, restoration, and reinvigoration unmatched by any Pennsylvania community. Bethlehem Steel became substantially involved in this process only after Chairman Arthur B. Homer, who had reigned as president and chairman for nineteen years, retired in 1964. Homer, who had been almost invisible in the community, immediately moved out of town. He was succeeded by Edmund F. Martin, a blunt, homespun steelmaker, who encouraged all steel employees to become more involved in city matters. His civic-conscious wife, Frances, a Moravian and a native of Bethlehem, undoubtedly was an influence in this regard, as was Laurence Fenninger, Jr., a Princeton-educated vice president, who became Martin's chief adviser on public affairs.

The point of this bit of parochial history is to show how

events rather than leadership brought Bethlehem Steel into the mainstream of the community where its management lived. Company attitudes to the town changed only when it was forced to reappraise old policies. Initiative was largely lacking. Not surprisingly, parallels emerge in Bethlehem Steel's responses to changing technology and changing markets.

Chapter 5

DIFFICULT YEARS FOR MEN OF VISION

I<small>T</small> is June 6, 1984. I am driving in the countryside six miles out of Appomattox, Virginia, and I think I am lost. The narrow tarmac road dips and winds through green, roller-coaster hills and there is no life in sight except grazing black angus. Suddenly, I see the mailbox I am looking for and I turn into a bumpy dirt lane.

Chickens scatter from the road as I pull up to a farmhouse where I see a man wearing overalls and soil-stained shoes coming out the door.

"I'm looking for the Robert Gray plantation. Am I close?" I ask.

"This is it," he replies. "Mr. Gray lives in the house at the bottom of this hill."

Ruts in the road get deeper and I have to navigate a washout that left a huge red gouge along the shoulder before I reach the house, a modest white clapboard bungalow. The front door looks unused so I walk around to the back. Sitting on the porch is a slightly wizened, white-haired man dressed in a white suit and a smart silk ascot.

He is Robert H. Gray, seventy-four, law school professor, accountant, and owner of twenty-seven hundred verdant Virginia acres populated essentially by several hundred gentle cattle. He is also the ex-steel executive who tried to redirect Bethlehem Steel, then the world's No. 2 steelmaker, from its mindless course, when it still had the money and market advantage to adapt to a swiftly changing world.

I had called Gray the night before. I wanted to know about Bethlehem Steel's short-lived Nassau operation—his brainchild, born and banished after one decade of operation in the 1950s. I had heard that Gray tried to persuade his superiors at Bethlehem Steel to lift their sights beyond the vistas of Saucon Valley and focus on the world beyond. That base in Nassau was to be Bethlehem's opening into the world. Why did it fail?

It was clearly painful for this man to discuss the past. But he did not duck the questions.

Gray came to work for Bethlehem Steel in a circuitous manner. He had left the Virginia plantation, which had been in his family for five generations, to pursue a legal career. His talents were recognized early by one of New York's most prestigious law firms, Cravath, Swaine and Moore, where he became an associate. An enthusiastic world traveler, he became convinced that American companies, with the exception of the oil firms, were blind to the forces bringing nations closer together and blinder still to the opportunities the changes offered.

Cravath assigned Gray to the Bethlehem Steel account, and he soon received an offer to join the company. He did so in 1946, becoming assistant controller and chief tax accountant. At Bethlehem, Gray found a supporter of his internationalist theories in Talbot Shelton, a Stanford-educated assistant vice president. Shelton had, in turn, the ear of both men's overall boss, Robert McMath, the vice president of finance and a powerful voice in the company's ruling cabinet.

Gray, the visionary, found a conduit to top management in Shelton. The two men became convinced of great opportunities for Bethlehem Steel if it could aggressively enter world markets before war-torn Europe and Japan rebuilt their mills. Further, Gray's study of the tax laws showed that profits from international operations, headquartered in a tax haven such as the Bahamas, could be recycled into other international investments; no taxes needed to be paid until the profits were returned to the home office.

The suspicion is that, when Shelton broached Gray's ideas to the board, the opportunity to circumvent punishing excess profit taxes, rather than any vision of international leadership, hit a warm spot. The directors approved the international venture, ignoring the carpings of in-house critics who insisted that Bethlehem was embarking on a plan that was either illegal, immoral, or at the very least, unpatriotic.

With a cloak of secrecy, Bethlehem Steel set up operations in Nassau late in 1951. William Humphries, who became vice president and controller of the new venture, purchased an office building across from the British Colonial Hotel in the best part of the city. Several houses were acquired for employees, and more than fifty people, including twelve from the home office in Bethlehem, staffed the company's new offshore world headquarters. No public announcement was made of the Nassau expansion, no mention of it ever appeared in annual reports, and even when Carroll Lovering, a top Bethlehem accounting officer, retired after a long career in 1984, the company's legal department ordered that a reference to his duty in the Bahamas be deleted from the news release.

The first piece of business in Nassau was to absorb Bethlehem's existing international operations—the buying and selling of iron ore, manganese, and other raw materials mined mainly in South America. Next, an insurance subsidiary named Overseas Underwriters Ltd. was founded with a London charter. "A beautiful idea," Gray describes it. "Reinsurance would spread the risk over several companies. Whoever heard of an insurance company going broke?"

At least twenty-one subsidiaries operated out of Bethlehem Steel's Caribbean office, according to the count of George Bannon, an accountant who set up the bookkeeping. Interocean and Marvin Steamship became the ore-carrying companies. Chartered in Panama and Liberia, their ships operated under foreign flags and therefore were free from oppressively protective U.S. maritime regulations and exorbitant wages demanded by the maritime unions.

The Nassau office became a major purchaser of ore, although not a single ton was ever shipped there. Bannon describes the transactions as follows: "Venezuela would sell ore to Bethlehem Steel, Canada—a subsidiary based in Nassau—at prices established by Bethlehem and U.S. Steel. Enroute to Nassau, the captain of the ship would be cabled and ordered to a designated port such as Sparrows Point [Maryland] or Lackawanna [New York], which then bought the ore from Bethlehem Steel's Nassau office."

Savings occurred because Bethlehem Steel was able to coordinate ore buying and shipping through an offshore company, Bannon says. Since all business was conducted outside the United States, profits were untaxed, "much like Eurodollars are today."

Shelton had envisioned a Nassau-based subsidiary that would buy steel from Bethlehem and resell it for the best price in the world market.

"That encountered too much opposition in the home office," Bannon recalls. "So we just sold it at a commission which, of course, was untaxed."

"We made money hand over fist," Humphries, the controller, said. "I know I signed over $400 million in checks. Granted it was in-and-out money, but for that time the profits were very large." So large, it appears, that Bethlehem created its own bank, chartering the Commercial Exchange Bank Trust in Curaçao and opening a holding bank in Nassau. The latter was named Gifford Bartlett Bank in honor of Bethlehem's then chairman, Eugene Gifford Grace, and its president, Arthur Bartlett Homer.

Indeed, the international subsidiaries flourished so hand-somely that Shelton was made a director of Bethlehem Steel. But the speed of his advancement did not sit well with rivals in the company's power structure, notably the hard-line oper-ations officials who thought Bethlehem should stick to making steel, instead of manipulating tax laws.

By the late 1950s, the aging McMath, Shelton's mentor, surrendered his chairmanship of the powerful finance com-mittee, ending his inner-sanctum support. Even though Shel-ton crewed on now Chairman Arthur Homer's ocean-going schooner *Salmagal,* and their wives were close friends, he could not avert a power coup. In fact, Shelton and his wife were on a three-week vacation in Hawaii with the Homers late in 1959 when the axe fell. Upon their return, Shelton discov-ered that Edmund F. Martin, the blunt, tough executive who succeeded Homer as president, had ordered William John-stone to shut down the Nassau operation. Shelton hastened into Homer's office, but he lost his appeal, and it was only a matter of time before he would also lose his job.

Shelton was shattered for reasons far greater than a per-sonal setback. Not only had an imaginative attempt at diversi-fying into international financial operations been halted, but so had the vision of Bethlehem taking a place in the world economy. Torpedoed with Nassau was a promising proposal that the company build a tax-free rolling mill in Belgium. The joint facility would have been manned by Belgian workers, but it would roll semifinished slabs purchased from Bethlehem's Sparrows Point plant.

Why did Bethlehem withdraw from the Bahamas so sud-denly?

"We needed the money here," Martin told me in an inter-view in 1985. "We weren't making anything from Nassau, anyway. We had to pay taxes on it all when the money re-turned to the States."

It is true that a recession in 1958 and a 116-day strike in 1959 had hit earnings hard. But Gray, who was treasurer of the Nassau enterprises, says he could feel opposition mounting from the home office well before the end came. Bethlehem's officers were not interested in international leadership or even diversifying.

Bernard "Bun" Broeker, who succeeded McMath in 1957, conceded as much in an interview in the summer of 1985.

"Bethlehem had a group of executives who were not prepared to relinquish offshore operations to an independent subsidiary in Nassau," he said. "Hell, the traffic vice president would come to lunch with a notebook in which he spotted where every ore ship was on a given day. Do you think he would permit Bethlehem Steel ships to take off and load at different countries without him knowing about it, much less without his permission?

"The Bethlehem board was not made up of men who would relinquish control. They came up in the business believing they controlled everything that was conducted in their area.

"My opinion was that Nassau would pass legal tests only if it were left to operate on its own. Because the board would not let it get out of its jurisdiction, we became an IRS target. I can recall a big roundtable discussion in which McMath said to Homer, 'You can kill Nassau if you want to, but I wouldn't.' We killed it because no one in Bethlehem was willing to let Nassau be independent."

At the end, frustration became so intense, Bob Gray says, that "I drank myself out of the company by 1959."

Gray became a law professor at Washington and Lee University, and licked his drinking problem soon after leaving Bethlehem Steel. From the porch of his Virginia home on that June day in 1984, Gray reflected on the aborted Nassau enterprise.

"I could get it started, but as soon as someone's turf was invaded, I ran into a stone wall. Nassau was a proper start. While they were complaining about our money rebuilding Japan and Europe, they did nothing about it." Referring to the Belgium offer, he said, "This was an opportunity to go into a devastated country and put up the most modern mill in the world. They weren't interested. Word would come back, 'We don't know anything about that country, so why try anything.' "

Robert Gray saw the company's future in steelmaking partnerships in Europe and elsewhere, arguing that the entire industry would be in trouble if it remained insular. Decades later, in 1984, David M. Roderick, chairman of the U.S. Steel Corporation, advanced essentially the same idea in proposing to import semifinished slabs from Great Britain as a means of saving his company's failing plant at Fairless Hills, Pennsylvania.

Had the American steel industry engaged in foreign steelmaking partnerships back then, Gray says, it not only would have had a diversified base but would have been in a strong position to resist the "outrageous concessions" to labor that are a factor in the current distress. The industry could have escaped being held hostage at every contract reopening, he says, if the union knew the American firms could fill customer orders by bringing in steel from affiliated firms abroad.

"Bethlehem Steel just wasn't interested," Gray adds. " 'Why rock the boat?' That was their favorite expression. 'We're doing well at what we're doing' was another. You'd talk about continuous casting and that sort of thing and they'd think you were crazy. There was leadership, but not entrepreneurship."

Gray says he sold his stock in Bethlehem Steel when he learned it was going to build a research center. "How were they going to make money on [more] research?" he asks. "There was so much research already done, and they weren't using it." His divesting was a visionary act. He sold his stock for $42 a share. Bethlehem stock was selling for around $17 during most of 1985.

William H. Johnstone, the vice president who shared with Gray the sense that Bethlehem must keep improving and changing its operations, had better luck in selling the company board his vision of Bethlehem Steel as a technological leader. With the support of Chairman Arthur Homer, the board voted Johnstone the funds to build a spectacular $10 million research complex high atop South Mountain, overlooking the city of Bethlehem.

Set in a dramatic courtyard, the research center became a showpiece. Bethlehem brought in about eight hundred engineers and support personnel to staff the facility, and research was elevated to an independent department, further underscoring the commitment. However, many skeptics questioned the wisdom of placing the center under a vice president, C. H. H. "Jerry" Weikel, who hadn't finished college and insisted on being addressed as "doctor" on the basis of an honorary degree.

Unfortunately, not much happened in Bethlehem's think tank. The new labs did improve the product mix, notably with the development of Galvalume, an aluminum-coated sheet metal, but did not produce the spectacular results such a massive investment of money should have provided. Or the technological leadership that Johnstone had hoped for.

Bethlehem approached the threshold of basic discoveries on several occasions, but major technological breakthroughs were prevented by in-house dissidents who raised challenges all-too familiar in the U.S. steel industry during the 1960s. "Why bother with this untested stuff? We're doing very well without it."

Continuous casting, a relatively recent innovation that is energy-efficient and replaces the costly ingot mold and primary rolling processes in steelmaking, is accepted today as a technological must for every modern mill. It was rapidly adopted around the world during the sixties, but not in the American integrated steel industry. The delay by the big steelmakers says much about why the industry is beset with technology catch-up problems today.

Bethlehem tried continuous casting in the 1960s in two separate experiments. In the first instance, a high-speed continuous slab caster, aimed at developing automotive sheet steel, was built in a pilot plant in the Bethlehem mill in concert with the Republic, Youngstown, and Inland Steel companies.

The experiment worked and news of its success spread at technical meetings. However, the pilot plant was abandoned by Bethlehem and its partners because it did not appear to be adaptable to the high volume required by the big steel firms. Yet as soon as the Japanese learned it was possible to make sheet slabs with this more efficient system, they picked up the concept and adopted it for high-volume production.

Subsequently, when an in-house study reported that refinements in continuous casting were developing rapidly and with expanding volumes, Bethlehem decided once more to go ahead with a full-scale continuous caster. But again narrow thinking ensured failure. A research team recommended that the continuous caster be built in a Bethlehem-owned plant at either Steelton, Pennsylvania, or Seattle, but the powers in steel operations instead dictated it be placed in the already cramped plant at Johnstown, Pennsylvania.

A four-strand caster, designed to produce bar, rod, and wire products, was 90 percent complete when it became apparent that the Johnstown site was physically ill-suited, as the research panel had warned. The entire project, on the brink of operation, was abandoned, and an investment of approximately $10 million went for naught.

At least one member of the study team, Mike Herasimchuk, the senior metallurgist, argued that the caster should be completed, problems and all, if only to gain experience with a manufacturing technique that would soon revolutionize steelmaking.

But his logic failed to sway the decision makers. The crucial technological developments in steelmaking would occur elsewhere, in Europe and Japan. By 1981, only 21.1 percent of the steel tonnage in the United States was made by continuous casting, while Japan was using the more efficient process to produce 70.7 percent of its output. The European countries were manufacturing 45.1 percent by continuous casting;

and even Canada, with 32.2 percent, had a better output than the United States.

Even in 1962, when Bethlehem made a daring decision to build an entirely new steel plant at Burns Harbor, Indiana— the last new integrated steel mill to be built in the United States—it was motivated more by its traditional wish to expand capacity than by desire to pioneer new techniques. Ten years before, a Bethlehem Steel team led by George Hurd had quietly purchased four thousand choice acres, including a stretch of beautiful sand dunes, along the Indiana shores of Lake Michigan for $12 million. When then-chairman Eugene Grace was asked what Bethlehem intended to do with it, he replied, "We didn't buy it for a bird sanctuary."

In one of industry's more enlightened compromises, Bethlehem surrendered the dunes area for a national park and received a deep water port, dredged by the Army Corps of Engineers, in return. The Burns Harbor plant gave Bethlehem a more competitive access to the Detroit area automotive market, and the gamble paid off at least for the short term. The increased capacity enabled Bethlehem to take advantage, in the 1970s, of the last remaining years of large consumption. Company profits soared to $342,034,000 in 1974, but that success is marred by the fact that much of the conventional equipment in the new plant was outdated almost from the start. A continuous caster was not installed there until 1975.

"We were making evolutionary changes when a technological revolution was going on," Dalton Brion, manager of primary processes research at Bethlehem Steel, laments today. Bethlehem never got its money's worth out of its research center, he says.

"So many things we developed were never taken advantage of," Brion points out. "Galvalume lay idle for years. The sensor lance was never appreciated until Tom Stott [vice president of steel operations] saw it in Japan. We had the lance first. There were no technical people in [top management]. It was almost like, 'Take the money, don't bother us.' "

Before building a continuous caster in any of its plants, Bethlehem plowed $35 million into putting up Martin Tower, the twenty-one-story office structure that tops all buildings in the area. The half-empty tower, which is now for sale, and the underutilized research complex, which is also for sale, stand today as stark symbols of the steel industry's blind commitment to monumentalism during an era when the company still had the resources to become a technological leader.

Sadder yet, the incremental technology being installed today—with increasingly scarce capital—to modernize Bethlehem Steel plants is rarely born of company research. The Bethlehem plant's major investment in 1985, its refurbished forty-eight-inch mill, features a seven-hundred-ton component shipped in from West Germany.

Chapter 6

THE YEARS OF SELF-DESTRUCTION

THE summer of 1959 started in Bethlehem with a searing heat wave, so hot that a reporter at the *Globe-Times* fried an egg on the sidewalk. People were also talking about the discovery of a mysterious, systematic siphoning of gasoline from the pumps at the city garage. And it was the summer of a contract reopening at Bethlehem Steel.

Of the three news items, the expiration of the three-year, basic agreement in the steel industry was of least interest to the town. Though nationally newsworthy, contract renegotiations had become an almost predictable ritual in steel communities. The steelworkers had struck in 1946, 1949, 1952, 1955, and 1956. Each time, after volleys of bluster from labor, management, and government, the strikes were settled by granting substantial wage increases followed by substantial rises in the price of steel. Then came wishful statements from Washington saying the administration was confident the new contract would not rekindle inflation—but in each of those years it usually did.

Residents of Bethlehem had no reason to believe that 1959 would be much different or, indeed, to suspect a calamity in the making. The strikes since World War II had lasted from one day to fifty-nine days. And since the strike of 1956 had run thirty-six days, most people thought that neither company or union had much desire for another battle so soon. The company, which always kept its white-collar workers on the payroll during a strike, certainly didn't want another confrontation. Meanwhile, after winning major gains in 1956, the United Steelworkers Union had no compelling reason to be pugnacious.

The reasoning turned out to be utterly wrong. First, a recession in 1957–1958 had shaken the industry's confidence. A short time before, the mills were selling all the steel they could produce. But steel production in the 1958 economic slump had fallen off to 85 million tons, the lowest since 1947. Serious concerns also had developed that the industry might have "given away the store" to the union in 1956. Besides having to sustain the generous annual raises, ranging from 9.1 to 10.5 cents an hour over the life of the three-year agreement, the companies also had granted the first annual cost-of-living escalator clause and new supplementary benefits.

However, the most ominous concession of all in 1956 had been a little-publicized provision in the contract. This is now known as the infamous Clause 2B. It stipulates that established labor practices cannot be changed unless there is a change in underlying conditions—an imprecise qualification that the union managed to interpret to its advantage. With the quickening tempo of labor-saving technology developing in Europe and elsewhere, steel company leaders began to realize that a clause locking in past practices was a terrible mistake. Not only could the clause block the adoption of new techniques, but it could make it impossible to improve old practices.

65

Encouraged by a new political climate, in which a Republican administration was in control at the White House for the first time in thirty years, the top eleven steel companies decided that 1959 was the year to get tough with the union. For the first time, they agreed to bargain as one unit, concluding that only a solid front could alter the union's pattern of steady gains that had started when 450,000 steelworkers struck the big companies back in 1946.

Early in 1959, a united steel industry sent forth a negotiating team headed by U.S. Steel's blunt R. Conrad Cooper, a former Minnesota football star. However, before the first offer was put on the table, U.S. Steel Chairman Roger Blough, accompanied by Cooper, called on President Eisenhower at the White House. They told him that runaway costs were crippling America's basic industry and that the major companies were willing to take a long strike, if necessary, to curb the situation. They appealed to the administration not to intervene. The pitch to the president, made by Cooper, is reconstructed as follows by steel labor negotiators who were at the meeting:

"Look, Mr. President, we are willing to pay the price. It's tremendously costly to take a strike. You have to keep your management work force intact, pay taxes, heat buildings, and all that. We are willing to do it, but for Jesus's sweet sake, every time we try it the government, which is supposed to be the referee, comes in and kicks us in the nuts. If you want us to get the costs down, if you want us to fight the union, okay, but stay the hell out when we do it. It's frustrating to take a long strike only to have you come in and conk us on the head and give the union the victory."

At the end of the pitch, Eisenhower asked the steel executives to send him supporting documents. Elated, Blough reported to the other industry chief executives that it was "a great meeting." Indeed it was. A few weeks later word came that the White House would not intervene.

Once negotiations began, Cooper demanded a freeze on

wages for one year. David McDonald, president of the United Steelworkers Union, avoided the expected sharp reaction, saying the union would not seek wage increases that would be inflationary; it wanted only a fair raise plus seniority changes. Both positions seemed so close that, after an appeal by President Eisenhower, the contract was extended two weeks after the June 30 deadline so negotiations could be completed.

Nearly everyone felt that an agreement was imminent. However, with the extension rapidly beginning to expire, negotiators became locked over something tougher than resolving wage increases. News stories began to report that the industry was demanding "contract language revisions in connection with automation and other technological advances." That meant the steel industry was holding out for the elimination or drastic revision of Clause 2B.

The union quickly equated that demand with a management attempt to eliminate jobs. Emotions at union hall escalated. In an eleventh-hour attempt to compromise, USW leader McDonald declared that the union was willing to agree that it was "not opposed to technological progress in the plants." Obviously that was far from a revision of Clause 2B. A negotiating year that began with so much hope suddenly deteriorated into what was to become the industry's most devastating confrontation.

The union struck across the country at midnight on July 15. Incited by the slogan "Man versus Machines," the steelworkers went into their strike formations the next morning. In Bethlehem, they picketed the plant entrances and paraded the streets in 90-degree heat. "They want to stretch out your work, take away your coffee breaks, and eliminate your jobs," speakers exhorted at strike rallies. Local union officers flooded their international headquarters with telegrams urging leaders not to give an inch on the past practice clause. No issue since the USW was founded fanned greater fervor among the rank and file.

The companies at first were confident that they could show

that widespread featherbedding, encouraged by Clause 2B, was sapping the industry. However, when it came to documenting their case, they stumbled badly.

Bethlehem Steel's vice president of Industrial Relations, George A. Moore, Jr., an easygoing veteran of the industry's negotiating wars, particularly recalls the frustrations of 1959 because, as a young attorney, it was the first year he was assigned to a bargaining team.

"I wish I could [figure out] how and why the industry walked into that clause in 1956 when three years later they were screaming, ranting, and raving about it," he says.

"We asked the companies to go into their plants and produce examples of featherbedding," Moore adds. One steel company executive complained about a hot metal crane operator—not identified—who originally had been assigned a man to relieve him every two hours because of the heat inside the cab; later, when the company air-conditioned the cab, the union refused to eliminate the relief operator job.

"Dammit, we looked all around the industry for that example and we couldn't find it. What we did find was that the supervisors who had been doing all the complaining kept no records," Moore says.

Featherbedding in the steel industry turned out to be as subtle as it was insidious.

"The big payroll padding was in the supplementary forces," one supervisor told me, admitting he was as guilty in perpetuating the padding as the union. "Remember, these practices were established at a time we could sell all the steel we could make. We exaggerated the labor force to make sure there was always somebody there to fill a job to keep the operations going. And we exaggerated the maintenance forces to make sure there was always somebody there to fix the machines. Once you add extra workers to get you through peak periods, the largest number that served on the work crew becomes locked in. Now it is past practice. The union's got you. It won't let you reduce crew size no matter how much production slumps or what labor-saving machines are added."

68

Determined to take a long strike over the issue, the industry nonetheless could not prove its contention with labor, the fact-finding boards, or even a good Republican friend in the White House. Self-interest kept supervisors from stepping forth and providing the facts that could have knocked out Clause 2B. Plant bosses chose to protect their work force for the day that production would pick up again. And who could blame them? The prevailing attitude always had been, "Let's stay ready for the big years." No one on top was telling the plant bosses to think differently.

The strike continued through the summer, and still no one became too worried. Steelworkers used their enforced vacation to paint and repair their homes while many wives worked to ease the financial pinch. By fall, however, the strike began to cripple the country. Automobile assembly lines shut down. Railroads were idled. Ore mines stopped operating and Great Lakes shipping came to a standstill. Workers in steel-dependent industries were laid off by the thousands.

While President Eisenhower continued to affirm his faith in the processes of the free enterprise system, many steel customers were less confident. They began scrambling to buy steel wherever they could find it, which meant scouting for supplies abroad. That was the year that steel buyers found out that other nations also sold steel; the buyers dealt first with the Europeans and then discovered the Japanese.

When the strike reached its 116th day, Eisenhower invoked the emergency powers of the Taft-Hartley Act and ordered the steelworkers back to the plants. However, extensive administration efforts, ranging from fact-finding to personal appeals by the president, failed to bring the sides closer. The eighty-day cooling-off period was rapidly running out and the union was certain to vote down the "last best offer" of the companies when Vice President Richard Nixon stepped forth.

President Eisenhower had left on a three-continent, eleven-nation peace mission in early December, leaving Nixon, a certain candidate for president in the election next year, to deal with affairs at home. No domestic problem was more compelling than finding a way to prevent the five hundred thousand uneasy steelworkers from resuming their strike when the Taft-Hartley injunction expired.

Operating offstage, as the newspapers reported, Nixon invited union leaders to his home one week and then entertained U.S. Steel's Roger Blough and other industry leaders at a pre-Christmas meeting the next week. He convinced the industry to change its "last offer" position. Then he set forth terms for a settlement that the companies grudgingly accepted.

The *New York Times* headlined the news on January 5, 1960, as follows:

STEEL SETTLEMENT IS REACHED

UNION VICTOR, PRICE RISE SEEN

NIXON, MEDIATOR, GAINS STATURE

The union won all it had hoped for, stretching its gains over other industrial workers even further. The wage increase of 8.1 percent was a bit lower than the rate of previous settlements, but the steelworkers blazed still another trail in benefits. The health and welfare plans, which previously were on a fifty/fifty basis, now became fully company paid. Retirement benefits were increased and accident insurance was liberalized. More importantly, the company lost its bid for relief from past practices under Clause 2B. The issue of work rule changes was deferred for study by a committee; no meaningful revision has occurred to this day.

If the settlement was good for the union, consider what it did for the political career of Richard Nixon. At the expense of the steel companies, he seemingly showed he was not a puppet of big business. Indeed, the settlement, so warmly received by the union, gave him badly needed evidence of loyalty to the working classes.

However, while the outcome of the strike was good for labor and helped Richard Nixon to the top of the Republican ticket in 1960, it was devastating for the industry. The 116-

day drought of steelmaking and the hefty price increases to pay for the settlement opened the door to forces that soon blew apart the steel oligopoly. Imported steel began streaming into America, from 2 million tons in 1958 to 5 million tons in 1959, marking the first time in this century that steel imports exceeded steel exports. Imports would never again return to the prestrike level.

Tom Crowley, a Yale graduate who became general manager of Bethlehem's Johnstown plant, recounts the subtle market changes after the strike.

"The big customers came back," he says, "but we began to lose the by-products—nails, field fence, and barbed wire. It was a nickel-and dime-impact at first but it started to affect the cost structure because we were now selling a smaller piece of the product.

"And soon we were competing with a market we could not match. Belgian barbed wire was being delivered on the docks at Baltimore at less money than it cost us to make it."

Don Thurlow, then an industrial engineer at Bethlehem's Sparrows Point plant, says that facility "was the first to be killed by the foreigners. Sparrows Point is on the water. We'd send a boat loaded with tinplate to Hawaii every month, twenty to thirty-five thousand tons. That stopped. The Japanese took [the business]. We used to send a couple shiploads of cold rolled down to the Gulf Coast. That stopped. The Europeans took it."

There's no doubt that imported steel eventually would have flooded this country once Europe's postwar rebuilding was complete and it became policy for many foreign nations to subsidize their steel industries. However, the strike accelerated the invasion. Even so, everything indicates that American steelmakers still thought old patterns would return, even as ships were unloading dramatically rising tonnages of foreign steel.

"They should have learned several lessons after the 1959 strike," says onetime steel executive Don Swan. "First, if there is cheap steel out there—even if it is only 5 percent of the market—it is going to impact on the price of the other 95 percent. Second, the strike showed there was a group of steel users looking to up their profit margins and this type of user discovered the cost benefits of foreign steel."

Meanwhile, the steady pattern of ever-rising steel prices and periodic shortages during the strike years invited an erosion of once-exclusive steel markets from a different direction. Minimills came on strong soon after the 1959 strike. These small mills make steel by melting steel scrap in electric furnace-continuous casting operations. They do not have the blast furnaces and coke operations to make the heavy structural shapes but, operating mostly with nonunion labor and adapting new technology, they zero in on selective products —and produce them with a fraction of the overhead of the giant integrated mills.

One of the pioneering minimills during this period was Florida Steel, which started out as a group of fabricating plants in 1956, buying structural supplies such as wide flanges and plates from Bethlehem's Sparrows Point plant.

"We saw soon that for us to survive we would have to produce our own raw material," says Edward L. Flom, who heads Florida Steel.

Florida Steel gambled on the electric furnace, converting scrap into steel though continuous casting. The integrated mills (with the exception of Japan's) viewed electric furnaces as having too low a volume and used them only to make low-tonnage specialty steel. Flom's firm was among the first to disprove the low-volume theory.

Florida Steel built an electric furnace at its Tampa plant and the first heat of steel was tapped in November 1958.

"The furnace was rated at thirty-five thousand tons a year. They told us we *might* turn out forty-five thousand tons. We made seventy-thousand," Flom says.

By the mid-1960s, such enterprising minimills as Nucor, which is today a Fortune 500 company, were thriving by adopting continuous casting, the technology that the integrated mills resisted until a decade later. Along with new production methods, Nucor introduced a new era of personnel relationships. The employee profit-sharing plan devised by E. Kenneth Iverson, Nucor's aggressive chairman, is a model for the industry, and has been a persuasive reason why Nucor employees choose not to affiliate with a union.

Among the first lucrative markets captured by the minimills were the small reinforcing bars used in great numbers for the nationwide highway-building program in the 1960s. Since reinforcing bars originally had no metallurgical requirement except tensile strength, they could be produced even in the most unsophisticated operations. As they refined electric-furnace steelmaking, the smaller producers began to beat out the big mills not only in supplying simple products but also more complicated ones.

"No one paid attention to the inroads of minimills," says Mike Herasimchuk, a senior metallurgical engineer for Bethlehem Steel. "One of my assignments was to keep abreast of them. I would periodically report what the status, the product, and the tonnage were.

"The response was, 'If a guy comes on stream with 60,000 tons of raw steel a year, let's not worry about that.' But one guy here and one guy there and pretty soon you see the old customers disappear."

Why worry, indeed. Bethlehem Steel produced a record 19,436,000 million tons of raw steel in 1964. Confidence in the Eugene Grace dictum was unabated. The corporate decision makers were confident that, as long as the company could expand capacity, profits would follow. They saw no reason to worry about the imports and minimills now nibbling at the market.

However, the forces set in motion by the 1959 strike were soon to overwhelm the steel industry from several directions. While the long and damaging confrontation had cooled the union's zeal to walk off the job, it had not lessened USW determination to make its members the highest paid in the world. Nor did it lessen the government intervention that kept forcing the industry to capitulate.

In 1965, it was President Lyndon Johnson's turn to assert the power of the presidency. A demoralized nation still felt the shock of the assassination of President Kennedy. People were growing uneasy over our deepening involvement in the Vietnam War. When a steel strike threatened to upset the country further, an angry Lyndon Johnson summoned the steel negotiators to the White House. An eyewitness on the management team who kept notes reconstructs the scene as follows:

"We are all sitting—four from the union and four from industry—in the Theodore Roosevelt room. Johnson is announced, 'Gentlemen, the president of the United States.' We all rise.

" 'Sit down! Don't give me that bullshit,' Johnson says. He is clearly on a tirade. He pulls out a paper. 'I have been fully briefed on this by the secretary of labor,' he says and turns to the right where the industry reps are sitting and goes at Cooper [R. Conrad Cooper, the U.S. Steel official and chief industry negotiator].

" 'Mr. Kupper, I want you to understand some things,' the president starts out. 'You tell those nickel-bending bastards you represent that if they try to bend that nickel on Lyndon Baines Johnson, I'll jam that nickel up their asses in more ways than they can count. You want me to build that lock at Soo Saint Marie [Sault Ste. Marie]. You can forget it. We just had an assassination. This country needs to rally behind my leadership. I've just been elected by the biggest majority since my political daddy, FDR. We are not going to have it fucked up by a goddam steel strike.'

"He then talks about steel's problems with the excess profits tax, trade enforcement, and other things—a master at leverage. Then he turns to where the union representatives are sitting.

" 'Now Mr. Abel [I.W. Abel, president of the United Steelworkers Union], I don't want to hear any bullshit from you. You represent a greedy union. You are out for all you can steal. You say you supported me in the election. What choice did you have? When I really needed you back in 1960 you went with Kennedy. You tried to beat me. After I became president, you supported me. What choice did you have?'

" 'You can't leave this room without a contract,' he says. 'I've got a platoon of the meanest, toughest Marines standing guard outside. They'll get you a cup of coffee or a sandwich, but you can't leave. I have TV time scheduled for Saturday to announce a contract. If you can't agree by then, I will tell the American public which of you greedy bastards is the worst.' "

The settlement came in the next forty-eight hours. The industry negotiators had intended to hold out for five cents an hour for the first year and three cents the next. They gave in at ten cents and six cents.

With each new contract, the gap in wage costs between American and foreign steelmakers widened and, in 1973, the big American steelmakers virtually ensured their inability to compete. They entered into a long-term, no-strike agreement with the union. An automatic cost-of-living clause was made a non-negotiable provision and a 3 percent annual wage increase sweetened the pot. In return, the union gave a no-strike pledge, leaving disputes to be settled by arbitration.

Known as the Experimental Negotiating Agreement, the compact was designed to mitigate the "boom or bust" cycles in steel by calming the fears of users during contract-reopening years.

"We and the union would tell ourselves after each settlement that we have to find a better way," negotiator Moore recalls. "The orders would roll in like hell up until June or May or whenever the contract was up and customers would also buy like hell from overseas to build up a hedge against a strike. Then afterwards, [if] the contract is settled without a strike we'd shut down operations, laying everybody off for about three months until they used up their inventories."

The ENA pact was hailed in many places as a breakthrough in the long history of hostile management-labor relations. However, it only accelerated the steel industry's distress. No one had foreseen the double digit inflation of the 1970s. The annual automatic cost-of-living adjustments (COLA) mandated by the pact became more lucrative than anything the steelworkers could have gained in contract-reopening years. Big Steel estimated that COLA added $2 per hour to hourly employment costs by 1977 and another $2.68 per hour by 1980. This largesse became even more punishing as companies continued their policy of passing equivalent salary increases to the nonunionized white-collar workers. Meanwhile, there were no provisions for increased productivity to offset these automatic pay escalations.

Ironically, many in the union protested their surrender of the right to strike during the term of this rewarding contract. Anticipating dissent from the rank and file, the steel companies even agreed to give each steelworker a $150 cash bonus at the time of signing and at each subsequent three-year renewal of the agreement. Reflecting on the bonus, J. Bruce Johnston, vice president of labor relations at U.S. Steel, remarked in a speech in 1976, "That's like my getting a free polio shot and then asking the doctor to pay me a bonus for taking it, because I gave up my right to get crippled. But we paid it, and we [will] pay again in 1977."

By 1977, with inflation unimpeded and the cyclical boom years no longer occurring, the steel industry was trapped in a devastating labor-cost bind. Even one of the principal architects of ENA pact, John J. O'Connell, vice president of industrial relations at Bethlehem Steel, urged it not be renewed beyond 1977.

"It isn't working . . . it isn't stopping the flow of imports," he argued. Nevertheless, the uneasy leaders of the industry, most of them remembering the scars of past steel strikes, chose to extend basic industry's most expensive labor contract.

Not surprisingly, American steel companies started posting red ink by 1977. In the case of Bethlehem, it was the first time in fifty years that the company failed to return a profit. By the time the no-strike agreement ran its course in 1982, steelworker earnings peaked at $26.29 an hour, counting the considerable fringes. Besides drawing the best wages in the industrial world, steelworkers now were protected with health care, dental care, eye care, and the security of supplemental unemployment benefits. They enjoyed the most liberal vacation plan in the industry, with the senior half of the work force taking company-paid thirteen-week vacations every five years, in addition to their generous annual vacations.

What's more, Clause 2B was still intact. At a time when even such technology-resisting unions as the International Typographical Union had bowed years before to automation in newspaper composing rooms, the United Steelworkers still managed to protect costly work practices. "Clause 2B was hard won and is therefore untouchable," the union contended.

All this is some distance from the days when the Mike Skertics were pounding steel for 90 cents an hour and dumping foundry dust on the state health officer's floor to win medical benefits for a consumptive steelworker. Many now say that the steelworkers have gone too far, that their excessive gains are the cause of today's deep distress in the industry. However, that conclusion ignores two other factors. One was the surrenders and misjudgments made by those in an excessively compensated top management. The other was the continued interference of government, which all but forced those surrenders to labor and abetted many of those bad judgments.

Chapter 7

STEEL AND THE
PRESIDENTS, AGAIN

AT 7 A.M. on April 10, 1962, the phone rang inside the Saucon Valley home of Edmund F. Martin, president of Bethlehem Steel. Chairman Arthur B. Homer was calling. Homer had a head cold and preferred not to preside at the corporation's annual meeting scheduled to start at 11 A.M. that day at the DuPont Hotel in Wilmington, Delaware. Would Martin mind subbing for him?

Martin, a square-faced man in his late fifties, could not refuse, but he had immediate reservations. This was not an emergency call to the plant where this veteran steelmaker had always been comfortable. This was a public appearance, and he was uneasy in public. Further, he did not know whether he could keep his temper under the certain badgering of John Gilbert, the minority stockholder activist who always appeared at Bethlehem's annual meetings.

Martin reined in his temper admirably while warding off numerous nitpicking questions from Gilbert. But then, with the formal part of the meeting ended, the steel executive met reporters for a press conference, where he dropped his guard.

"The industry and the United Steelworkers Union signed a two-year contract five days ago. Can the nation expect a price increase?" a reporter asked.

"Hell, no, this isn't the time to raise prices," Martin replied with characteristic frankness. "We should be trying to reduce the price of steel, if at all possible, because we have more competition, particularly from foreign sources."

From World War II to 1962 the steel companies had had ten price increases, always marking up prices after each labor settlement. The press understandably interpreted Martin's comment as an indication that the industry was breaking out of the old pattern. The story was significant, and the wire services gave it wide play.

Martin had barely returned to Bethlehem that afternoon when a stunning radio report came out of Pittsburgh. U.S. Steel, the nation's No. 1 producer, had raised prices by $6 a ton. Astonishingly, Bethlehem, despite Martin's statement, followed the next day with a price increase for the same amount. Before that day ended, half of the twelve largest steel firms had raised their prices.

When the news reached the White House, President John F. Kennedy was furious. He thought he had a firm promise from Roger Blough, U.S. Steel chairman, that there would be no price increases. His secretary of labor, Arthur Goldberg, had worked long and hard backstage to end the inevitability of the old steel strike-steel price-hike scenario. He was convinced the outcome of steel negotiations would be a major factor in wage-price stabilization throughout the economy. Goldberg, who had been chief counsel for the United Steelworkers before coming to the White House, had managed to persuade USW president David McDonald and the union bargaining team to accept a modest package for labor, the cost not to exceed projected gains in productivity. Both Kennedy and Goldberg insisted it was tacitly understood that the steel companies, in return, would not raise prices.

The new price spiral, coming right after Martin's statement, set off a presidential tirade. An angry Kennedy at this time made his famous remark, "My father always told me that all businessmen were sons of bitches, but I never believed it until now."

With his hopes at least temporarily thwarted, Kennedy launched a public offensive against the steel giants, using Martin's statement as a means of getting back at Blough. Attorney General Robert Kennedy promptly brought his office into the battle by announcing a price-fixing investigation. "Because of past price behavior in the industry," Robert Kennedy said, "the Justice Department will take an immediate and close look at the current situation and any future development."

Late that night, two men flashing FBI identification visited Martin's home and rang the bell. "I came out and these guys were presenting their FBI cards, saying they wanted to know what I said at the meeting," Martin recalled in an interview.

A few miles away, Marshall Post, the Bethlehem Steel media aide who had set up the press conference, was routed from bed by the FBI at 4 A.M. A number of reporters who had covered the conference were also visited in the predawn hours. By noon, U.S. marshals were delivering subpoenas at the main offices of Bethlehem Steel and U.S. Steel, ordering appropriate officers to produce pricing records before a federal grand jury in New York.

This high drama was to became moot in the next twenty-four hours. On the following day, April 13, Inland Steel, the fourth largest producer, announced it would not raise prices. Bethlehem Steel then rescinded its increase and, within hours, U.S. Steel did the same.

The steel price controversy of 1962 is today a textbook case. It is still debatable whether Kennedy's outrage benefited or harmed the nation, since an aura of antibusiness bias subsequently haunted his administration; this aura was cited by many as a psychological factor in part responsible for the economic slump soon to come.

However, in my view, the actions of Bethlehem Steel in this episode provide a case study of another kind. The company, after a half decade of rule by the strongest men in the industry, saw its top executives exposed in this 1962 showdown as mere followers of U.S. Steel. This was hardly consistent with the company's legacy of independent thought and action, which had inspired *Fortune* magazine in 1941 to describe its management as "the smartest of the major steel producers."

Edmund Martin's gut reaction that steel prices should not be raised was right on target. Not only was competition threatening from new foreign mills built with American post–World War II aid, but the steel companies had finally won the noninflationary labor terms they had been demanding. The contract that had been produced with Kennedy administration persuasion contained no wage increase for a year and the new fringe benefits amounted to 10 cents an hour per man, a cost that reasonably could be expected to be made up by the 2.5 to 3 percent improved productivity which was then the trend in the industry.

Had Bethlehem's chairman, Arthur B. Homer, and his board had the courage to back Martin in his honest reaction to a new round of higher prices, they well might have led the way in applying a check on the self-destructive wage-price pattern. Instead, Bethlehem's actions made the public suspect that big steel companies were out to get more than they deserved. Meanwhile, the USW also cried "double cross," saying it would have demanded higher wage increases had it known the steel firms intended to raise prices as usual. So the already deeply rooted hostility between labor and management became even more entrenched.

Bethlehem's ruling powers not only failed to back a top officer voicing the courage of his convictions, but chose to obfuscate Martin's remarks. Company statements suggested that Martin was misquoted at Wilmington. "Mr. Martin was in fact indefinite about the matter of prices. He indicated that the future increase in labor costs is unfortunate at a time when we were trying to hold the price line," read a Bethlehem press release.

When the storm was over, "s.o.b." buttons mocking Kennedy's outburst were passed around the Bethlehem boardroom. Officers wore them on their lapels as badges of honor. But, while the companies after a decent interval did raise their prices selectively, they nonetheless never again risked White House disapproval by imposing massive across-the-board increases. They resorted instead to discrete increases.

There is a postscript to this episode. In an interview at his office in the Hotel Bethlehem during the summer of 1985, I asked Martin, who retired in 1972, what he really did say on that eventful day in Wilmington in 1962. "I said, 'Hell, no, this isn't the time to raise prices,' " Martin replied. Why had he kept quiet when the company was suggesting he was misquoted? Martin simply shrugged his shoulders. I can conclude only that he was too much of a team player in 1962 to make an issue of his personal conviction.

It would be too easy to lay all the blame on Bethlehem's top officers for the company's sad retreat and other serious executive misjudgments yet to be made in the crucial 1960s. But any search for factors behind the decline of leadership in Bethlehem must start with the two men who built the corporation—Charles M. Schwab and Eugene G. Grace. For all their greatness, neither trained successors to fill the vacuum when they no longer could lead.

Schwab, a classic example of the American rags-to-riches story, started in the industry as an unskilled laborer. He rose to the presidency of Carnegie Steel in twenty years and then became the first president of U.S. Steel. A famous falling-out at U.S. Steel led the freewheeling Schwab to strike out on his own, breaking away from the company that controlled more than 50 percent of the steelmaking in the United States. He founded Bethlehem Steel in 1904 by acquiring a little iron company in Bethlehem, an iron ore mine in Cuba, and seven other minor facilities.

Schwab built Bethlehem into a strong company largely because he was the only steel producer who had the courage to mortgage his future for a new type of mill to make structural beams—wide flange shapes that were stronger and cheaper than the old riveted girders. The towering skylines of many American cities are today testimony to Schwab's vision. The other steel companies adopted the innovation only after he proved that it worked.

The gregarious, adventurous Schwab was not to be tied down by day-to-day management. Soon after coming to Bethlehem, he found a production genius in young Eugene G. Grace and put him in charge of running the mill. Grace, a reserved, calculating electrical engineer who graduated at the top of his class at Lehigh University, was appointed president of the company in 1913 at the age of thirty-seven.

Schwab, the entrepreneur, and Grace, the professional manager, built Bethlehem into a steel colossus. From a small company in 1905 with an ingot capacity of 213,000 net tons —not even 1 percent of the national total—Bethlehem became the world's second largest producer by World War II with an ingot capacity of 11,850,000 tons, about 14 percent of the national total. It had major steel plants at Sparrows Point, Maryland; Lackawanna, New York; Johnstown, Pennsylvania; Steelton, Pennsylvania; and, of course, Bethlehem, where it also maintained its main offices, and its shipyards flourished on both coasts.

Bethlehem's growth was tied into an incentive system from which its top officers profited handsomely. More than a few people wondered about its excesses, however, when·in 1929 Grace received a bonus of $1,636,000; his bonuses averaged about $500,000 a year thereafter, regularly making him the highest-paid corporate executive in America. And, of course, other key executives shared in the bonus pool proportionately.

When Schwab died in 1939, the company became a one-man show. Grace's administrative style meant keeping a finger on everything that went on at Bethlehem. His production genius ensured Bethlehem's rapid expansion of steel-making capacity at a time when the mills sold all they could produce. But his close-fisted leadership, although good for profits, created an environment that was hardly conducive to grooming successors or accommodating alternative views. Because his word was gospel on all matters, no one gained entry to Grace's inner circle by being even a courteous dissenter.

Grace was seventy-nine and ailing but still very much in charge when I became editor of the *Globe-Times*. His friends would sometimes tell me fanciful stories about how Grace, who once was a scratch handicap golfer, still shot his age. No one was fooled about his fading physical condition, but even when Grace became bedridden, his word prevailed in the boardroom. Any decision of any consequence had to pass the test of whether the action was what "Mr. Grace" would want.

When a series of strokes in 1957 finally rendered Grace incapable of ever again going to his sixth-floor office, the board of directors, all Grace appointees, had to face an inevitable decision. The company had gone as far as it dared without a leader. The directors agreed Grace must be persuaded to step down as chief operating officer. But who would break the news to him?

Norborne Berkeley, a vice president and golfing companion who was known to concede Grace three-foot putts, was designated as spokesman. He visited the bedridden chairman at his sprawling mansion on Prospect Avenue, then known as "Bonus Hill," and told him that his friends on the board thought he should lighten his responsibilities. Grace is said to have been agreeable to the notion.

He became honorary chairman soon afterward and held the title—with bonuses intact—until he died in 1960 at age eighty-three. Grace never designated a successor. The post went virtually by default to Arthur B. Homer, a shipbuilder, who was chosen because he had been president during Grace's last years. His mild personality most likely persuaded his colleagues he would lead with the least disruption of the old order. Homer, who was already in his sixties and regarded by many as the weakest contender, succeeded Grace as chairman on October 1, 1957. Edmund F. Martin then moved up the ladder to become president.

The two new officers had the all-but-impossible job of filling the vacuum left by a half century of Schwab's innovation and Grace's patriarchial style. The company promptly tried to polish up the image of its new leaders by bringing in Maxeda von Hess, a speech coach, to teach them the basics of elocution.

But Grace's successors had far more than personal image to worry about. The patriarch's system had created a company divided into tight departments headed by vice presidents accustomed to being answerable only to the man at the top. They were extremely protective of their ground. No craft union within the steel plant was any more sensitive to encroachment. Naturally, this rigidity was hardly conducive to an open exchange of ideas when overall corporate decisions had to be made.

John F. Heinz, a Brown University graduate who became a speechwriter for Bethlehem's top executives, enjoyed insider status despite his lack of an impressive title. He was appalled at how Bethlehem's inbred system stifled independent thought even a decade after Grace's death.

"The definition of intelligence or ability was to do things the Bethlehem way," Heinz remarked. "And the Bethlehem way was 'The way we always did it in the past.' " This mindset hindered the company even up until 1983, Heinz maintained, when he ended thirty years of service by taking early retirement and moving to a different company.

Interviewed during the spring of 1985 in Chicago, where he had begun another career as Inland Steel's manager of corporate relations, Heinz described the Bethlehem system this way: "The characteristic that each department had in common was that they were fiefdoms, going way back. The turf was inviolable and prizes did not go for objective intelligence or academic training. Rarely were promotions based on merit."

Junior executives could best plot their progress by looking at the senior members ahead of them on the departmental ladder. They moved up a rung when someone above them died, retired, or moved out. There was no fear of being passed by someone younger but smarter, short of committing a grievous offense. The most unpardonable sin was offending a high-ranking steel officer socially, especially at Saucon Valley Country Club, where I noticed that respect for rank was asserted even in the men's locker room where ranking officers received shower priority. Another liability was a wife who drank too much, talked too frankly, or showed any independence. However, up until the time of the industry's distress, an offending executive was rarely fired. He simply was moved into a corner away from the flow of action and out of sight of his boss.

Meanwhile, vice presidents competed with one another for approval at the top, sometimes in ways that had little to do with steelmaking. In 1960, Heinz recalls, word went out that, in the best interests of the company, Richard Nixon should defeat John Kennedy. Other corporations passed the hat for the Nixon campaign, but Bethlehem established a quota. The company not only set an amount expected from each management-level employee, but some departments enforced the collection with threats.

Heinz said the minimum expected contribution to the Nixon campaign in his public affairs department was $25 a person. Russell Branscom, then the company's vice president of industrial and public relations, told his top lieutenant, William Jess, to accept nothing less than 100 percent participation.

"I gave [the money] to them with a little bit of moaning," Heinz, a Kennedy admirer, recalled. "But a friend down the hall, also a Kennedy supporter, just refused to [contribute]. He ended up sitting in Bill Jess's office and the whole staff felt for both of them. Bill, who was embarrassed, would say, 'I'm sorry but we are all expected to make a contribution.' There would be silence. Then Bill would say, 'I wish you would give it very serious thought.' More silence. Then the two of them just sat and sat and sat.

"Branscom did not accept anything except 100 percent," Heinz said. "He wanted his department to present an impeccable record to the top."

Yet Heinz admits that doing things the Bethlehem Steel way, in those days, still achieved excellent results for those who judge companies by the bottom line. Profits during the 1960s averaged about $130,100,000, despite the jarring Kennedy confrontation year when profits slumped to $88,-678,000. While Bethlehem Steel executives kept insisting that annual earnings were below those of other manufacturers when computed on the basis of comparative investment, I never could accept that reasoning. I wondered what the real profits would have been during this era had the company brought its salaries into line, cut featherbedding, and eliminated many extravagances.

If Bethlehem's profit picture still belonged with the best, its social conscience during those years belonged with the worst. Bethlehem Steel, the other large producers, and the United Steelworkers Union would pay dearly for their resistance to the social reawakening occurring in America during the 1960s.

Chapter 8

BETHLEHEM STEEL'S GÖTTERDÄMERUNG

Bethlehem Steel is the archetype of the U.S. industrial image . . . if Bethlehem exhibits all the virtues of private capitalism, it also exhibits its defects. In terms of the social responsibilities of modern American industry, Bethlehem's management is provincial. Socially, they are like characters in a majestic Götterdämmerung.
—from *Fortune* magazine, April 14, 1941

UNFORTUNATELY, the author of the *Fortune* piece quoted above was so impressed with the industrial achievements of Bethlehem Steel ("a well-integrated company with plants that have a steel capacity equal to the production of the United Kingdom") that he did not document his observations about social shortcomings. Only when the Civil Rights Act of 1964 forced all major American industries to look at their social deficiencies did the public get an understanding of Bethlehem's failure in this regard.

The Bethlehem Steel I knew in 1964 was lily white in attitude. While only about one thousand blacks lived in Bethlehem, a city of seventy thousand people, many of their forerunners had come here long before the flood of immigrants arrived from eastern Europe. The first blacks found jobs as housekeepers and gardeners on Bonus Hill, but their children were hired by Bethlehem only for the filthiest and most arduous jobs. Most endured quietly for the future of their own children, hoping to educate them so they could move out of this tight community of no ghettos but unscalable walls.

The conditions at Bethlehem's huge Sparrows Point plant in Maryland were perhaps the worst. Sparrows Point is located about where the Mason-Dixon line falls. But there is no doubt on which side the company thought it belonged. Here about 7,300 blacks were part of the plant's work force of 22,300. When I toured Sparrows Point in the early sixties I was appalled to see "white" and "colored" toilets, separate locker rooms, and even "white" and "colored" drinking fountains. The tolerance of this policy not only provided an insight into the conscience of the company but also suggested the United Steelworkers Union was a partner in discrimination. I wondered how much support a black could expect from his union if he filed a grievance.

No major company dependent on federal contracts was more vulnerable than Bethlehem to the sweeping changes that engulfed the nation after passage of the Civil Rights Act. Out of it came an executive order empowering the government to require that all such firms follow nondiscriminatory employment practices. Yet no company could have been less aware of the act's implications than Bethlehem Steel.

The first public suspicion that Bethlehem would resist fulfilling its social responsibility occurred on March 17, 1964, when the *Globe-Times* reported the disquieting dismissal of a company manager. Philip B. Woodroofe, supervisor of municipal services, was sent packing when his superiors found he was one of several local citizens organizing the Community Civic League, a nonprofit group seeking to improve racial relations in Bethlehem.

Woodroofe, a tall, gentle man who was forty-five at the time, was the son of an Episcopal minister. He had served in World War II as an Air Force officer and later became director of residence halls at Lehigh University. The father of three college-bound daughters, Woodroofe seized the opportunity to increase his earning power when Bethlehem Steel sought a manager for its municipal affairs department in 1957.

Woodroofe was an enthusiastic supporter of civic causes. His wife, Nell, worked as a volunteer for educational and charitable institutions. They were a family sensitive to the times, and I came to know them well. Soon after becoming editor, I hired Nell's talented mother, Ruth Hutchison, to do art and music reviews for the *Globe-Times.*

I could readily understand how the Woodroofes, both committed members of Trinity Episcopal Church, were among the first to be motivated by a letter to all Episcopal churches early in 1964 urging parishioners to involve themselves in their communities to forestall civil rights problems. The racial riots that started in Birmingham, Alabama, were certain to spread north. By helping to organize the Community Civic League, the Woodroofes believed they could address areas of tension before they erupted.

When he learned of Woodroofe's role in the civic league, the aforementioned Russell Branscom, the vice president of industrial and public relations at Bethlehem, went into a rage. He stormed into the office of Ivor Sims, vice president for administration, demanding that Woodroofe be fired. True to the way things were done at Bethlehem, Sims, long a team player, agreed to back Branscom's demand.

In their eyes, Woodroofe had committed two unpardonable mistakes. He had failed to clear his volunteer work with the company: it mattered not that Woodroofe considered this activity personal; Branscom insisted the public would consider the manager a spokesman for the company. Secondly, by becoming involved in a "community" project, Woodroofe had wandered from "municipal" affairs, a department under the domain of his own boss, General Services Manager Frank Rabold, and now was trespassing in "community" affairs, which came under the authority of the turf-conscious Branscom.

Rabold could see he was in a power struggle, but he was not secure enough to oppose the joint demands of Branscom and Sims. He knew when he was outranked. But he did try to save face for his department by calling Woodroofe into his office and delivering his own ultimatum: quit the Civic League or face the consequences.

Woodroofe tried to explain the mission of the league, pointing out the first meeting had been held in the house of Mayor Gordon Payrow (a Republican) and included leaders of the city's Catholic and Protestant churches, as well as leaders of the black community.

Rabold was unswayed, pointing out that nothing short of resignation from the league would satisfy Branscom.

Woodroofe argued that it would be embarrassing both to the company and the Community Civic League if he quit now, virtually on the eve of a meeting in which he was to be formally seated with the other founding directors. Would it satisfy the company if he withdrew and instead substituted Mrs. Woodroofe's name on the ballot?

"Rabold felt it was not acceptable—not only to substitute Mrs. Woodroofe's name on the ballot but [he said] she should not be associated with the organization, and this would be as disagreeable to the company as my own name being associated with the organization," Woodroofe wrote in a memo filed afterward.

"I then indicated that I felt I should not remove myself from the Community Civic League and I would have to suffer the consequences of defying a dictum from higher up," Woodroofe stated.

Woodroofe's conversation with Rabold occurred on a Saturday. When he reported for work the following Monday, Rabold told him, "I'm surprised you're here."

"Do you mean to say I'm really through?" Woodroofe asked.

"Yes, you're through," Rabold replied.

The *Globe-Times* editorially criticized the firing. Citizens expressed outrage in letters to the editor, some containing the boldest public criticism of the company yet seen in this steel-dominated town. The *New York Times* sent Joseph Loftus, a first-rate reporter, to cover the story, and the dismissal became a national issue. Letters of support, and even checks, flooded the Woodroofe mailbox. Other letters of protest went directly to the steel company.

Officers at Bethlehem Steel were quite conscious of who was or was not supporting the Woodroofes. There was never an open threat of reprisal, but there was never any doubt that the powers on top would note who was disloyal and "take care" of them through promotions denied or, in the case of community critics, through business contracts withheld. As a result, the Woodroofes found themselves shunned by several intimate friends. Even the pastor of Trinity Church, which was heavily supported by Bethlehem Steel executives, never uttered a word of support in their defense. However, the pastor's superior, Episcopal Bishop Freckerick J. Warnecke, did write the Woodroofes a forthright letter saying "the church is honored by your stand."

Most who recall the incident feel even today that the firing was motivated by racial prejudice at the upper levels of Bethlehem Steel. Woodroofe never claimed that. When I interviewed him in the summer of 1985 I asked him, in reflection, why he thought he had been fired.

Newly retired as a real estate executive in Philadelphia, Woodroofe said his assessment had not changed. He is certain he was caught in a power struggle between Rabold and Branscom. Nevertheless, there was an unmistakable trace of sorrow in his voice as he shook his head, reflecting on how in those turbulent times the company was more concerned about soothing "stupid, petty men" than helping avoid racial tension.

This incident bares one more rigidity at Bethlehem Steel: the wave of civil rights protests did move north, and did engulf the company. Once more, Bethlehem was forced to battle problems because it had failed to recognize symptoms.

Problems arising from discriminatory employment practices first erupted in Bethlehem's Lackawanna plant, where 2,100 blacks worked among the force of 13,900 people.

George Moore, the attorney for Bethlehem's industrial relations department, who was sent there at the outset, describes how the investigation started: "Some guy in the personnel office at Lackawanna gets pissed off or gets fired and he goes to the Justice Department and discloses to them that for summer replacements, all the superintendents' kids, all the general managers' kids, and all the foremens' kids get these jobs. In fact, he says there is a golden list and when they decide to put some people on, they go to the golden list.

"The Justice Department came in like a herd of turtles, and the next thing we know this thing has expanded way beyond the summer bit. They are now starting to concern themselves over all our employment practices and suddenly we have the first major civil rights case in this area. And then CORE [Congress of Racial Equality] wants a piece of the action."

CORE, the shock troops of the civil rights revolution, was noted for such tactics as chaining demonstrators to chairs in segregated restaurants to achieve their goals. Its members came to Bethlehem in a caravan of buses, alerted the press and TV, and headed for Bethlehem Steel's main office.

"You would think we're under attack," Moore says. "I meet with the chief of police and our security people. We establish markers out there where the CORE gang is not supposed to cross. Keep them out of the building. No one is going to talk to them. That is the plan. That *was* the plan. The first thing they do is get into the revolving doors. Now they are in the lobby. Now we got to meet with them. So I get stuck and go down."

The suits were more than the company's legal department could handle. The New York law firm of Cravath, Swaine and Moore was retained to deal with the flood of discrimination cases.

"We have the courtroom plastered with computer printouts [showing black vis a vis white statistics]—that's the only way you can prosecute or defend a class action civil rights case," Moore says. "Then the case also became a private class action suit brought by activist lawyers. Remember this was the 1960s generation of young lawyers. You went into their office and you sat on the bare floor. I couldn't believe it. Here is our blue-blood law firm from Wall Street cast into this bloody mess."

The wave of demonstrations and class action suits quickly spread to Sparrows Point. Moore describes the scene:

"Next, CORE targets Baltimore to get more P.R. The *Sun* papers don't love us anyway, and they give them the space. CORE marches around the plant and then they go down to the Department of Labor in Washington. And they march up and down demanding that the secretary of labor meet with them. The undersecretary meets with them on the steps, in front of TV cameras, and makes all kinds of promises."

By now Bethlehem Steel was under siege from all directions. On January 17, 1973, the government launched an all-out assault. The company became the largest industrial facility ever ordered by the Labor Department to correct discrimination against minority workers or face cancellation of all federal contracts. Secretary of Labor James E. Hodgson, who issued the order, stipulated that Bethlehem correct a seniority system that "has been found to perpetuate the effects of past discrimination in the assignment of blacks to jobs and departments with limited advancement opportunities."

Fortunately, in Moore's view, the government soon after targeted U.S. Steel for discrimination at its Birmingham, Alabama, plant. Up until then Moore could not manuever because the suits were only Bethlehem's problem. With U.S. Steel now under government heat to make corrections, the entire steel industry was put on notice.

"It forced us to open a dialogue," Moore says. "The rest of the industry began to say, 'It's you today, it's us tomorrow. We can't live with this.' Not only were legal expenses adding up, but each judge was coming in with a different concept of what is a fair seniority system."

Moore became chairman of the steel industry committee

to negotiate a system that would comply with the civil rights laws. That meant restructuring the whole seniority system, with about 450,000 employees affected.

There is nothing more touchy in the steel industry than seniority. That blacks were held back was not denied, but coming up with a remedy that afforded them special leapfrogging privileges to compensate for past discrimination was something that, at the outset, sorely affronted the United Steelworkers Union.

The plan had to correct inequities in the promotions and hiring, not only of blacks, but also Hispanics and women. Searching for a formula became a nightmare. Every suggested change was certain to rub a sore spot somewhere.

"We met with the union for three months," Moore says. "And we had to keep going back to the companies—each had its own seniority system no matter what the [industry-wide] contract said. And the chief executive officers kept insisting, 'Not one penny for retribution.' "

Late in 1973, the joint union-industry committee finally presented a plan to Washington. Until then, Moore says, he had been naive enough to think there was one government in the Capitol. He discovered there were at least three.

"At the first meeting, it was the Justice Department and the Labor Department. Then there was the Equal Employment Opportunities Commission [EEOC]. A new guy by the name of Powell [John H. Powell, Jr.] was coming up for Senate approval as chairman of the EEOC. While we're trying to work things out down here, he's up there on the Hill making all kinds of statements on what he's going to do to all those industry discriminators. Meanwhile, it's clear Justice is losing jurisdiction."

The joint union-industry committee met with all three groups at the beginning, but the EEOC kept dropping out of the discussions, insisting that the talks could not proceed until the steel companies agreed to the issue of back pay. Justice and Labor seemed more interested in modifying the seniority provisions so workers were not dead-ended.

"Six months later, we're still at it," Moore says. "You talk about intrigue and clandestine moves. We would meet each weekday until 3 or 4 A.M. By Monday, when we returned from the weekend, nothing was good. The EEOC would come in and kick over the traces. Nothing was good because they hadn't been part of it."

Eventually, Justice and Labor capitulated to the EEOC. They went along with its demand that the steel industry agree to back pay for victims of discrimination. A formula was negotiated between the government and the industry, and Federal Judge Samuel C. Pointer, Jr., eventually granted two consent decrees, one covering white-collar workers and the other covering the blue-collar ones.

But other plaintiffs were waiting in the wings. "We took the decrees down to Judge Pointer and they were entered at 11 A.M.," Moore says. "By noon the Legal Defense Fund and NOW [National Organization of Women] had filed two separate lawsuits to overturn [them]. They could not have read the decrees that fast. They were getting this thing blow-by-blow out of the negotiating room."

The consent decrees were not overturned. Instead, the steel industry satisfied the government by agreeing to the most expensive civil rights settlement in history. The nine steel companies consented to pay $30.9 million in back wages immediately and about $25 million more in the next two years to about forty thousand minority-group workers in 255 facilities. This amounted to an average payment of $700 in compensation for the amount each minority worker was underpaid during the previous two and a half years.

Further, the steel companies also agreed that one-half the future openings in skilled jobs would be filled by minorities and women until their numbers equaled their overall percentage of employment in each plant.

"We got every big steel company in the boat except one," Moore says. "That was Inland Steel. They were run by Block [Joseph L. Block] and they felt they were the most liberal of all and would be damned if they were going to be held up.

Give the United States Steelworkers Union credit. They agreed to pay $5 million, in effect conceding complicity. Inland also eventually contributed but only on the condition that their share be used for education and retraining and not be construed as payments for past discrimination."

A final glitch occurred when Bethlehem began to implement its settlement. "We couldn't get a definition out of the Justice Department or EEOC on what the hell is a Spanish-American," Moore says. "We were ready to pay the Puerto Ricans, but we also had a lot of Portuguese. Nothing was in the settlement about them, but we reached in our pockets and paid them, too."

Bethlehem learned its civil rights lesson the hard way. The company, which ten years before fired a manager for beginning a group to improve racial relations, now provided in George Moore a leader who cut through a maze of seniority contract-clauses and found the basis for making amends for past insensitivity.

And the American steel industry, renowned for its arrogant protection of self-interest, provided the government with its biggest impetus ever to end such discrimination in all other industries.

Chapter 9

OMINOUS SIGNALS AND NO QUICK FIX

N the summer of 1974, when President Gerald Ford was
in the White House trying to soften the shock of Richard
Nixon's sudden abdication, the steel industry appeared safe
and well. The big mills were in the midst of a record profit-
making year and employment was at its fullest. The only dis-
concerting vibrations felt in Bethlehem were the in-house
murmurings heard in August when Bethlehem Steel picked
Lewis W. Foy as its sixth chairman.

Succeeding Stewart S. Cort, a Yale-educated marketing
expert, as the chief executive of Bethlehem Steel was a heady
rise for Foy, fifty-nine, a silver-haired, low-key manager who
had only a partial college education. But Foy stood for the
traditional American values, and showed that someone could
still come up from an obscure job in a plant to the top post
of the nation's No. 2 steelmaker.

Four years earlier, Foy's elevation to the presidency, the
company's second highest office, from a position as vice presi-

dent of purchasing stunned many observers because of his limited exposure to the actual manufacturing process. Foy started as a laborer in Bethlehem's plant in Johnstown, his home town, but left to enlist in the army in 1941. Separated from the service as a captain after the war, he rejoined Bethlehem and was assigned to purchasing, where he remained for twenty-five years. Then, almost out of the blue in 1970, he succeeded Stewart Cort, the president who moved up to chairman when Edmund F. Martin retired.

Foy's smooth looks and engaging smile masked an interior toughness, but that hardly explained his surprising selection to lead the company. In an informal moment, Chairman Cort was asked by a friend why he picked a man with such limited steelmaking experience as his successor.

"Lew always had an interest in all phases of the business," Cort replied. "He was a tough bargainer. He had a hell of a lot to do with the important equipment and labor contracts that were required to build Burns Harbor [Bethlehem's billion-dollar integrated mill in Indiana erected during the 1960s].

"At one point we had sixty subcontractors and five thousand workers on the site. That required a lot of contractual work. Lew always seemed interested in the legal side that went along with the contracts. He made sure that nobody took Mother Bethlehem."

Then Cort cited one more Foy quality—he didn't drink, or at least he didn't drink hard liquor. As an executive who sometimes reveled in excess (at times embarrassingly so), Cort consciously or not left Bethlehem Steel a leader with one quality that he could never claim.

Foy assumed the leadership of Bethlehem Steel as all the chairmen had done before, confident in the wisdom of the company's well-paid managers around him and secure in the growth-mode thinking that had brought Bethlehem bigger and bigger profits.

And why not? Bethlehem's earnings in 1974 hit a record $342,034,000, up from $206,609,000 in 1973 and more than double the $134,584,000 it had earned in 1972. An expansion program started by his predecessors was running full tilt. Burns Harbor was mushrooming, with a new slab caster being installed that year, and the world's most modern bar mill was to be in place at the Lackawanna plant by 1975.

Besides, such acknowledged steel experts as Father William T. Hogan of Fordham University were projecting a strong demand for steel in the decades ahead, forecasting that the industry would have to boost capacity to 190 million net tons by the 1980s, a big step up from the 165 net tons prevailing in the mid-1970s. McGraw Hill's *33 Magazine,* a trade publication for metal products, devoted an entire issue to the anticipated demand, stating, "Virtually everyone concerned with the steelmaking industry is plagued by a single, overriding question, 'Where are we going to get the additional capacity to satisfy the demand for steel by 1980?' "

That was August 1974. Within the next two years, the steel industry's rosy world suddenly turned gray. Foy, who came into power when the industry was on its last big whirl, was suddenly faced with pulling Bethlehem out of an economic tailspin. He inherited a crisis that had no quick solutions. The forces unleashed by the 116-day steel strike of 1959, the years of lavish blue- and white-collar raises, and the steady and often arrogant price increases could not be stopped.

Foy often stressed that inquisitiveness was essential for success in business. Had he, and the other industry leaders, truly used this quality they could have seen danger signs all around them. While they were blindly accepting the need to increase capacity, the marketplace was signaling the opposite.

In fact, had the steel companies been even slightly inquisitive about the marketing concerns of their good customers, such as the Jorgensen Steel service center near Philadelphia, they could have sensed a clear message of crisis ahead.

Jorgensen, one of the nation's largest supermarkets for steel, sells to contractors who do not order from the mills directly—because they do not want to stock inventories or require only standard steel shapes that service centers can keep on hand. Earle M. Jorgensen, the wiry Scandinavian who founded the business in 1921, had a long allegiance to Bethlehem Steel. The company helped him survive a depression and reorganization by "carrying" him when other companies shut off his credit. Now chairman of a New York Stock Exchange–listed business with twenty service centers in the continental United States and Hawaii, Jorgensen—and his executives—tried to stay loyal to Bethlehem when cheaper, sometimes even better steel began flooding in from Europe and Japan in the 1960s.

"When I started with the company as a salesman in 1969, we wouldn't admit we were buying foreign steel," Thomas J. Pohl, assistant general manager at Jorgensen, recalls. "To accommodate some customers who insisted on it, we would buy minuscule amounts and call it File 27. If you wanted service, you would say, 'Do you have any File 27?' "

Pohl said Jorgensen resisted as long as it could, but by 1974 even his company had to bring foreign steel out of the closet. "We were always ones to support domestic mills, but our philosophy changed," Pohl says. "It had to. Competition. We could no longer ignore the price advantage."

Steel bars shipped all the way from Japan were found to be of comparable or superior quality—and 15 percent cheaper. Sheet and coil, basic for the East's automotive jobbing shops and computer cabinetmakers, came in at $60 a ton under the domestic price. Meanwhile, neither Bethlehem nor U.S. Steel could be competitive with minimills furnishing the popular 2 X 2 quarter angles that go into framing and scaffolding. The integrated steel mills simply stopped making them.

The major steel firms nonetheless refused to undercut each other's posted prices. Soon loyal customers started to disappear. The mills warned many of them that they would lose preferred service when a tight market returned. But customers chose to gamble on foreign steel in numbers that the domestic industry never imagined.

The United States moved from a position as the world's

leading exporter of steel to its largest importer. U.S. imports increased from 3.3 million tons in 1960 to a high of 21.1 million tons by 1978, according to the findings of the Steel Advisory Committee directed by Dr. Timothy P. Roth and commissioned by the U.S. Department of Commerce.

Complicating the situation, overly optimistic estimates of the growth in steel demand after the last boom of 1973–1974 not only led to erroneous decisions to expand domestic capacity but also inspired developing countries to build showcase steel mills.

New steel complexes appeared in Brazil, Mexico, Korea, and Taiwan, many of them built with low-interest loans arranged by free-world interests eager for the business. Many of the governments involved then attempted to insulate their industries from market pressures through a steady flow of subsidies, and further protected them with trade restrictions against American imports. The subsidies severely depressed prices globally and greatly increased import penetration in the United States.

Problems came from still other flanks. The aftermath of the energy crisis of 1973 brought a totally unforeseen setback to the steel industry. When the automotive industry, to meet new fuel-efficiency standards, embarked on a crash program to build smaller cars, the average American car, which weighed 3,850 pounds in the midseventies, shrank to 2,800 pounds by the 1980s. Lighter materials—plastics and aluminum—permanently reduced the use of steel on dashboards, bumpers, and fenders.

Add to the changing automobile picture the impact of changing life-styles, with fresh and frozen foods replacing canned foods, and beer and soda drinkers buying their beverages in aluminum cans, and the negatives for big steel became staggering.

Obviously, all the upbeat projections of steel demand turned out to be completely inaccurate. Not only did demand fail to grow, but western world-steel demand actually declined. American steel mills were now losing market share in a dwindling market.

With the situation ever-worsening, the American steel industry, abetted by faulty government forecasts, still clung to the premise that new boom years were around the corner. As late as July 1979, after red ink already had ended nearly fifty consecutive years of Bethlehem Steel profitability, Lewis Foy was trumpeting this theme.

"Make no mistake about it, the market for steel is growing," Foy declared in a keynote address at the time. "The Department of Commerce released a study that concludes as follows: 'The domestic steel industry will require a net addition of 12 percent, or 21 million tons, by 1990 if it is to continue to supply 85 percent of the United States consumption.' "

The fact was that the industry needed retrenchment and modernization, not expansion. In subsequent chapters, I will deal with the painful human and economic dislocations that resulted when hard realities finally became apparent. However, no account of this 1970s era, which some too easily dismiss as the start of the deindustrialization of America, can be put in perspective without the views of Bethlehem's chairman at the time.

Lewis Foy retired as chief executive officer of Bethlehem Steel in 1980 at age sixty-five. But he was still keeping regular working hours when I interviewed him during the summer of 1985 at his office in the Hotel Bethlehem.

"There are so many common-sense things that could have been done to prevent the disaster this country is now in with its basic steel industry," Foy said. "The industry made a helluva lot of mistakes. And now I am talking about our own company. We didn't keep ourselves lean enough. In hindsight, we never should have built Martin Tower [Bethlehem Steel's twenty-one-story main office building], because once you build a building you fill it up. We permitted costs to escalate. We never should have created in-house all of the services that we did. We tried to be all things to all people. We never should have done that."

With those admissions out of the way, Foy sat upright and placed his arms on the desk. In an almost apologetic tone, he blamed the U.S. government as the greater villain in the steel crisis. His argument ran thusly:

First, the government, invoking antitrust powers, placed a harsh burden on Bethlehem Steel by its refusal to permit a merger with Youngstown Sheet and Tube in the 1950s. To position itself for a share of the automotive and construction markets shifting to the Great Lakes area, Bethlehem therefore was forced to build a new plant at Burns Harbor. This required the expenditure (some investment analysts called it the squandering) of more than a billion dollars of capital to erect facilities that it could have obtained in a Youngstown merger.

Then, there was the tough attitude that the government took on steel pricing. "It was always a battle," Foy said. "There was really no justification economically for the battle between government and steel—simply because steel is such a small part of the gross national product. It's always been something less than 2 percent, and yet the position always taken by the government is that whatever steel did set the pattern for the country [The government did not look] at the long-range position they were putting the industry in. . . .

"Other industries had a far greater impact on the economy, such as food and computers. You never heard of them being attacked by the government for prices. And yet they are so much more involved in the total economic picture than steel."

Other problems that government created for the steel industry in the 1970s, Foy maintained, were the stiff environmental mandates requiring enormous capital investment to meet standards that often were unreasonable. For example, the industry was given a deadline to clear up emissions from the coke ovens when no technology yet existed to do the job.

Unlike U.S. Steel, which simply fought controversial environmental regulations in court, Bethlehem Steel under Foy's leadership did all it could to comply. The company spent an estimated $543 million since 1974 for pollution control equipment, much of it to meet excessive and even conflicting rules.

"The U.S. steel industry, because it is an aging industry, as contrasted to Japan and the rest of the world, had to retrofit all of the environmental [hardware] that came into being in the sixties and seventies, taking up about 25 percent of our capital money for that period," Foy said.

"We should have been permitted to write off expenditures for environmental purposes the year they were made and not be forced to treat them as just a regular expenditure for depreciation over a period of twelve to eighteen years. Do you know how [depreciation] operates in other countries—Canada for instance? They write it off the year it's made. The longest depreciation in any other country I know of is three years."

The pollution cleanup of Bethlehem plants became a model for the industry. By the mid-1970s, as I drove to work at the *Globe-Times*, which is three blocks from the fenced-in steel plant, I noticed women hanging out wash in backyards within its shadow, something they would not have attempted before a $5.5 million baghouse, a facility to filter dust-laden emissions, was installed.

At Sparrows Point, in Maryland, the cleanup of the red dust from the Bethlehem plant brought enthusiastic comments from neighbors. Thomas Colbert, who operated a gas station there for twenty-seven years, told the *Bethlehem Review*, the company's employee publication, that for the first time he no longer had a problem cleaning reddish-brown deposits from the windshield of his car. And water quality at Bethlehem's Burns Harbor plant bordering Lake Michigan was deemed so safe that the Indiana Department of Natural Resources began to use the plant's pier as a stocking area for trout and salmon.

But the heavy outlays for pollution control without offsetting tax depreciation advantages devastated the company's cash flow, severely restricting the capital needed to modernize facilities. "Think how we could have helped ourselves if the government would have given us a break on depreciating equipment faster," John Jacobs, a former vice president of steel operations at Bethlehem, remarks. "[Is it] any wonder Japan and Europe were so far ahead of us on continuous casting?"

William J. Tattersall, a Bethlehem Steel attorney who left the company to become deputy secretary general of the International Iron and Steel Institute, reinforces the complaint. "From my international perspective," he says, "no other country in the world, even Japan, ever made its steel industry comply with such strict demands on clean air and clear water. On top of that, no other steel company in the world, with Japan a possible exception, has to comply with the health and safety requirements demanded by our government."

Foy insists that, despite the shackles imposed by government, the American steel industry did an exceptional job of modernizing. He feels it has been unfairly maligned. He produces figures compiled by steel analyst Peter Marcus showing that for the last ten years the United States required the fewest man-hours in the world to produce a ton of steel. "That doesn't happen unless you modernize," Foy says. "The hooker is that the numbers that killed us were these [the hourly labor costs that prevailed during his last full year as chairman in 1979]: U.S., $16.39; West Germany, $13.55; Japan, $9.73; United Kingdom, $6.68.

"You put this hourly compensation cost together with the inflated dollar, and it just wipes out any advantage you have. The point is that we would not have had those low man-hours for a ton of production if we had not spent billions to modernize—which we never got credit for."

Foy shakes his head and goes on to the industry's next complaint.

"I suppose the one thing I never expected—and have been amazed at—was how the small undeveloped countries, and some not so small, were able to get world financing to build additional steel capacity when it was obvious that the world's capacity was excessive. The financing came from the Export-Import Bank and people like that. They permitted them to build these damn steel plants in the face of a world glut." (The Steel Advisory Committee estimates that the glut has grown to 200 million tons of excess global steelmaking capacity.)

Foy does not volunteer to discuss the one question that stands out in any examination of decisions made by the steel industry in the 1970s, so I put it to him directly.

"What took you so long to recognize that American steel was in trouble?"

"I don't know how to answer that," he replies. He goes on to describe the company's extensive efforts to monitor imports, to document the case for government action against dumping of foreign steel, and the successful fight, which he led as chairman of the American Iron and Steel Institute, to convince the government of the need to combat dumping.

Foy is too much of a Bethlehem team player to speak frankly on this sensitive subject. I got a more perceptive answer some time later, when I went to Chicago to visit Jack Heinz, Foy's former speechwriter.

"I think Foy recognized he wasn't getting the information he really needed, and so he went out and hired Don Trautlein from Price Waterhouse in 1977," Heinz says. "Boy, a lot of old faces just disappeared fast after that."

So did many sacred-cow notions. Whether Foy intended it or not, his legacy was to bring the man into the company who would be the most resented and ruthless chairman in Bethlehem's history, but also the man most determined to save the dying American steel industry.

Chapter 10

THE SINKING
OF THE FLAGSHIP

B Y the early 1970s, some executives were beginning to think the unthinkable in the board of directors room at Bethlehem Steel. Until now, it had been assumed that the company would always continue operating its key plants, upgrading them as necessary, but never actually shutting down a big facility. However, accelerating negative forces were changing such comfortable assumptions.

Yet, no outsider could have guessed that the first Bethlehem operation proposed for elimination, in early 1975, would be Fabricated Steel Construction. How could the company, in its pursuit of wage concessions, even suggest closing down the technically sophisticated fabricating shops, or dismantling the internationally-acclaimed engineering group? The fabricators were Bethlehem's flagship division, builders of such national landmarks as the George Washington and Golden Gate Bridges, and of such famed office buildings as Chicago's Merchandise Mart and New York's Waldorf-Astoria.

Leaders of the United Steelworkers reacted with disbelief; among the rank and file, there was much mocking laughter. But Bethlehem management stuck to its guns, insisting the entire fabricated steel division would be closed unless the company received concessions from the union. If the management was to be believed, the jobs of about six thousand employees in six fabricating plants across the country were at stake.

On the surface, all signs suggested the company was bluffing. It had finished 1974 with a record profit of $342,034,000. However, hindsight shows the union made a colossal error in doubting Bethlehem's sincerity. Had the union looked closer it would have seen that big steel fabrication was becoming a classic victim of the nation's changing economy. Fabricating had become an intensely competitive business.

The decline was all the sadder because Bethlehem's fabricators had been a great American success story. In 1931, Chairman Charles Schwab saw a way of challenging U.S. Steel, and in its own lair. He bought the McClintic-Marshall Company, an established fabricator with plants on the West Coast and in the Pittsburgh and Chicago areas, the heart of U.S. Steel territory.

At the time, the country was mired in the Depression and capital was scarce, but Schwab and Eugene Grace gambled that the nation was on the threshold of a building boom of high-rise offices, suspension bridges, power-line towers, and all else that long had been neglected. Not only would their new fabricating subsidiary compete with U.S. Steel's fabricators for the business, but it would provide an outlet for many thousands of tons of Bethlehem's Steel in marketing areas long dominated by the rival company.

McClintic-Marshall, in business since the turn of the century, had already made a reputation in office building and bridge construction. Bethlehem was content to operate the company under its original name until Grace, in keeping with his administrative style, visited San Francisco in 1936 to see the Golden Gate Bridge.

"Bethlehem did a good job of construction," Grace is said to have remarked to a foreman at the site.

"Bethlehem?" said the puzzled foreman. "Bethlehem had nothing to do with it. McClintic-Marshall built this bridge."

Grace changed McClintic-Marshall's name as soon as he returned home. It had been known as Fabricated Steel Construction, Bethlehem Steel Company, since that time. Grace thought so much of its potential that he made the fabricating division a major beneficiary of substantial investments during the pre–World War II years.

Much of that investment was made in Pottstown, which is strategically located near Philadelphia, with easy rail and truck shipping-access to New York City. Pottstown became the largest of Bethlehem's fabricating plants. Its work force of seventeen hundred was equipped with shops that could move beams, plates, and angles up to 116 feet long through spacing tables that could automatically stop the materials for punching holes for riveting or bolting at any designated place, thus assuring precision-drilled beams and frames for assembly at the site. Working with hydraulic presses and towering cranes, Bethlehem's skilled craftsmen fitted and assembled steel for the original and extra decks of the George Washington Bridge, the central office building of the Chase Manhattan Bank in New York, and the National Gallery of Art in Washington, among scores of other jobs.

Bethlehem's fabricators earned a reputation for ingenuity. The plant at Leetsdale, Pennsylvania, on the banks of the Ohio River, could produce gigantic bridge sections, so large that Bethlehem had a built-in edge on competition. Only at Leetsdale could those huge sections be built on a river bank and launched on the spot into a navigable river. This capacity to transport whole sections without using roads or railroads enabled Bethlehem to win huge contracts.

Bethlehem built new fabricating plants at Torrance, California, in 1955 and at Pinole Point, California, in 1965 in anticipation of the West Coast building boom. With the long-established plants at Bethlehem, Pottstown, Leetsdale, and Chicago, the company put together a formidable fabricating network, challenged only by American Bridge, the U.S. Steel subsidiary.

"We had absolutely the best technology in the fabricating business," says James T. Gearhart, a retired Bethlehem Steel vice president who came up in the company by handling fabricating sales. "In 1965 to 1967 everything was completely consolidated and rebuilt to accommodate the welding market, which had pretty well taken over from the bolting operations. Rhett Maxwell, an expert in welding operations, was given free rein to put us in step with what the market now demanded. We developed plant and equipment to handle large, complicated members, which enabled us frequently to negotiate projects on a preferred-cost basis."

Projects built on a preferred-cost basis meant that Bethlehem could build with a minimum of risk. The company earned this preferred status because the nation's largest contractors knew that Bethlehem's total capabilities reduced their own risks. They would often negotiate a contract with Bethlehem that was higher than other bidders but, in their view, worth the extra money for the security of having Bethlehem do the job.

"The best of the building contractors knew that their making money depended on the erection of steel," Gearhart says. "If they got an erector who was dependable and produced on schedule, that was more valuable to them than anything else."

Besides, Bethlehem's resources enabled it to weather the many financial uncertainties that frequently ruined the smaller, independent fabricators. "It takes a lot of money to handle any job," Gearhart explains, "because first you purchase the material, then fabricate, and then erect. So you might have steel tied up in a job for a year before you get the first payment . . . and even a government project can be risky. We built a railroad bridge over a river in Tulsa for the Army Corps of Engineers. Then Congress didn't appropriate the amount of money we had agreed on."

But times changed, and so did Bethlehem's dominance. First, construction labor-rates in the late 1960s escalated, forcing contractors to look hard for ways and places to cut costs. Labor costs increased at such a rate that they pushed prices beyond the point that anticipated income could justify the contract. As a result, Gearhart says, contractors started to skimp on steel by changes in design practices.

"We found less redundant bridge structures. The ability of the designer and his computer to slim down a project resulted in some pretty flimsy designs at times, which is something we had to be concerned with. Instead of including excess members to pick up the stress when one member exceeds its limit, computer-designed bridges are built closer to accommodating actual stress. That saves steel but also increases the chances of catastrophic failure."

Meanwhile, runaway construction costs also increased contract defaults. This hurt Bethlehem in one more way. "So many bonding firms began taking over jobs that they began to insist that companies let contracts only on firm prices or at least the minimum exposure to escalation," Gearhart says. "That put the gamble in the fabricator's hands."

Those firms or government agencies who could afford to let preferred status contracts became fewer in number, and Bethlehem, the total fabricator, found itself slipping fast as a competitive bidder. While the expertise of its engineers always had been a big plus, the overhead of maintaining a large engineering force, as well as hundreds of permanent draftsmen, now became a severe liability. Bethlehem found itself losing jobs to independent contractors who expanded their capability—and lowered their costs—by using engineering consultants and independent draftmen only as long as there was a job to do. And by entering into joint ventures with other small fabricators, the independents found a way to raise the financing to compete against Bethlehem for even the major jobs.

More ominously, Bethlehem saw the gap widening between its wage-rates and those of its competitors. The company's fabricating employees were covered under the master contract negotiated by the United Steelworkers Union and the major steel companies. Every raise and benefit won for workers who manned the steel plants was automatically passed along to the fabricators.

By the early 1970s, Bethlehem's fabricators were making about fifteen dollars an hour. According to Jack Dakes, an assistant to the general manager in the fabricated steel division, a study showed that Bethlehem was paying "three dollars an hour higher than the main competition and sometimes seven and eight dollars higher than the nonunion competitors."

As in the steelmaking plants, fabricating productivity also was hampered by Clause 2B, the provision that protects past practices. "It was common to see a job where two or three guys were standing around because of work rules," says William Heil, a former draftsman in the Pottstown plant. "In beam fabrication, one guy would come along and set up the location of the angle, the other guy would come along and tack-weld it, and a third guy would be needed to check it. In a nonunion plant, one guy did all the work. There wasn't the luxury of doing one particular job."

Heil, now a partner in an independent drafting shop, was no less critical of the management waste he observed in his twenty-five years at Pottstown. "Management had too many people on the payroll who couldn't do their jobs," he says. "When a guy couldn't handle it, they just shifted him over and created another job for him. They never fired anyone and I know clerks who made $30,000 a year . . . . The thirteen-week vacations [every five years] for workers were ridiculous, but remember management got seven-week vacations every year and something called a tonnage bonus. The shop would be losing money, but they got a bonus if the tonnage improved. Ever hear of an incentive like that?"

The suspicion that Bethlehem Steel was becoming a dinosaur in the fabricating business began to dawn in 1970 when the company bid on the contract for the $600 million, twin-towered World Trade Center to be built in lower Manhattan. Bethlehem bid $117 million, barely beating out the only other bidder, U.S. Steel's American Bridge Company, which came in with $122 million.

There was great elation at Bethlehem headquarters. However, congratulations had hardly died down when the sponsor of the buildings, the New York Port Authority, announced it was rejecting the bid. Bethlehem's figure was nearly 50 percent above the Port Authority's own engineering estimates. At the same time, the authority filed a price-rigging suit against Bethlehem and U.S. Steel.

The court suit never came to trial, but Bethlehem lost what it thought would be a whopping contract. The trade center later was built by a consortium of contractors put together by Malcolm Levy, the Port Authority's chief of planning and construction. He broke down the steel fabricating work into segments and invited new bids. They came in at $83 million, only slightly above the authority's $80 million estimate. The work was let to fifteen fabricators, many of them cutting their costs by using foreign steel. At least three of the successful bidders were as far away as the West Coast where—believe it or not—they bought Japanese steel, fabricated it in their shops, shipped it to New York via the Panama Canal, and *still* were able to meet the Port Authority's price.

The loss of the World Trade Center contract was shattering. Bethlehem could not recover the estimated $500,000 spent on engineering and estimating work that went into preparing the bid. Further, its engineers had substantial input into the design of the twin towers, now a Manhattan landmark, but did not receive a smidgen of credit.

Robert Linn, the Port Authority's deputy director for physical facilities, concedes that many of the new design concepts were tested with Bethlehem experts before being adopted. "We would bring [people] in from Bethlehem and U.S. Steel to answer questions about what was possible. We wanted to make sure the design did not have anything that the fabricators would be incapable of doing. We kept picking their brains. It made a difference how the building was designed. They were very close to the project and that is why we were so shocked by the bids."

Doubts about Bethlehem's ability to compete as a fabricator multiplied. "Litigation began to pervade the industry," Gearhart says. "I remember a guy from Allegheny Power walked in to visit our chairman, Stewart Cort, just to tell him that they were suing him for $7 million over delays supposedly caused by us in erecting towers for Keystone Public Power. We showed that the failure of their own engineers in providing necessary information caused the delays. We won the suit but still had to defend it. And the personal liability problem began to loom as a threatening thing for corporate executives. We had a couple of cases where top executives were accused of being responsible for the death of an employee.

"Because we were big, we were held responsible for the acts of the owner, the designer, the authority, and everyone else even though we might have been the fourth steel erector. When you add this potential risk to the cost in estimating a job, you lose the bids. We lost the bid on the approaches to the Verrazano Bridge that way. We did build one of the [bridge] towers and manufactured most of the cables on the suspended structures, but we lost big jobs because we knew we just could not lay off the risks on the insurance company."

The most crushing suit occurred after Bethlehem erected the spectacular suspension bridge between Jamestown and Newport in Rhode Island. Construction of this $61 million, two-mile span across Narragansett Bay started in 1968 with announcements that revolutionary new techniques would be used.

Under a system developed by Bethlehem's engineers,

erectors were able to build the bridge by pulling sixty-one wire strands at a time from anchorage to anchorage instead of one or two at a time by the conventional method. *That* was a stunning achievement. Unfortunately, under another system developed by the designer for the bridge, all structural members were coated with a rustproof epoxy, thereby theoretically making the painted surfaces of the bridge virtually maintenance-free. *That* was a stunning failure.

The paint began to peel off in sheets even before construction was finished. "The problem was that the guy who devised the coating system did not provide for a proper bonding to the steel," Gearhart says, blaming the designer. However, the Newport R.I. Bridge and Tunnel Authority would not accept the explanation. It took Bethlehem to court in 1974 and after a trial that lasted thirty weeks, the company was ordered to pay a $5 million judgment.

The World Trade Towers and Newport bridge setbacks were demoralizing, but no less worrisome were the mid-1970 marketing projections. The interstate highway program was over, virtually ending the building of the big suspension bridges for which Bethlehem was famous. The interconnecting power transmission systems had been built. The high-rise office markets were shifting to the south and southwest, increasing the company's shipping costs. On the West Coast, fabricators were using Japanese wide flange steels, $40 to $50 a ton cheaper, and killing domestic competition.

In late 1974, Gearhart was named to a Bethlehem team called together to consider the future of the fabricating division. "At this point we were still profitable," he says. "The wage gap did frighten us, yet we felt that we could live with the disadvantage if it remained constant. But when we charted [the gap] for five years ahead, it then was so wide that there would have been no chance to compete. There was no way to close the gap, either, because the union refused to remove the fabricating employees from the basic contract."

Early in 1975, the message was delivered to the union: take

a 10 percent pay cut and a two-year wage freeze in the division or Bethlehem Steel would close Fabricated Steel Construction. For the average fab worker making $15 an hour, that would have meant $1 an hour less in his paycheck and a cut of 50 cents an hour in benefits.

Cries of outrage reverberated in union halls and fabricator shops: "The company is bluffing," "We heard those threats all before," "How could they close this plant with all that investment?" Meanwhile, the USW leadership abetted the resistance, stampeding "No" voice-votes and in some instances shutting out the rank and file from any vote at all.

"What happened down here was pathetic," recalls Heil, the draftsman in the Pottstown plant, who points out that he had grievances with the company but deplored the union's actions. "The union got those guys together and said, 'Do you want to take 10 percent off what we have been fighting for all these years?' The answer: a resounding no! A lot of them were convinced Bethlehem Steel would *never* close down the Pottstown plant."

Company and union officials met in negotiating sessions at the USW headquarters building in Pittsburgh. B. Bruce Dunwoody, a Bethlehem vice president who was then assistant general manager of fabricating, recalls going up in the elevator for a negotiating session. "Two union men who didn't know who I was started talking. 'To hell with them,' I heard one say. 'They [the fabricators] are only 2 percent of our membership. If we give in, everybody else will be after us.' [The unions] were not about to jeopardize the basic agreement in the steel industry."

Lewis Foy, then Bethlehem's chairman, gave his fabricating operating officers and the union officials three months to reach an agreement. "Do you know what they came up with?" Foy told me. "The union said it would give up the dental plan. The only concession they would give was the dental plan. When they brought that to my desk, I said, 'Shut it down.'"

Thus ended the first concessionary bargaining in steel industry history.

All the plants were closed by the third quarter of 1976. Some were sold in part, some were rented, but not a fabricator could be found to continue even partial operations in any of Bethlehem's six plants.

When I visited the desolate Pottstown plant in the summer of 1985, I was greeted by a large billboard, "Pottstown Industrial Complex—Space Available." The huge shops that produced so many of America's bridge and building landmarks were largely unoccupied, their corrugated sheet sides deteriorating and their rail tracks overgrown with weeds.

I looked up Paul Shaner, sixty-five, a small, slightly stooped man who spent his lifetime working at the Pottstown plant and served as treasurer of the union, USW Local 2177, for six years before it disbanded. Sitting on a lawn chair in front of his neat home on North Hills Road, Shaner told me closing "the fabs" was a tragedy." He blamed three factors: "First, the company. When things were going good they gave the union everything they wanted and then didn't know what to do when things went bad. Then the government. It stopped putting up money for highways and bridges. And the union. They didn't believe the company when it said it would go out of business." He said he couldn't recall whether the union ever gave workers in Pottstown a vote on the decision to reject the concessions.

How would he advise the steelworker locals being asked for concessions today? "I would tell them you're better off working. But I was never a radical."

Bruce Dunwoody, Bethlehem Steel's vice president of manufactured products, views the closings from another perspective. "We lost for this country one helluva resource," he says. "We had physical capability and people-skills that will just never be put together again. If someone wants to build another Golden Gate Bridge or another Minute Man missile silo, all of which we did, they are going to have trouble. Joint consortiums just can't pull together all of the technical and physical resources to do a job like that efficiently."

"Wouldn't it have been in the country's and your interests for Bethlehem to continue carrying the overhead?" I ask.

"We had that philosophy for too long," Dunwoody replies. "That's what got us into trouble."

American Bridge Company, the nation's other total fabricator, also had to live with wages and benefits mandated by the United Steelworkers' basic agreement. It lasted only a few years longer. U.S. Steel closed all eleven American Bridge plants by 1984 and put its engineering and erection services up for sale in 1985.

Chapter 11

BETHLEHEM'S BLACK FRIDAY

IT had already been a tough winter for Lackawanna, the Bethlehem Steel plant town just south of Buffalo on the shores of Lake Erie. Nearly fourteen feet of snow had fallen during the first three weeks of January 1977. Then, on Friday, January 28—a day that started cold but clear—a new storm, with blinding snow driven by winds of up to seventy miles an hour, swept in across the lake.

The blizzard lashed Lackawanna unmercifully for the next three days, bringing zero temperatures and burying the area under as much as twelve feet of fresh snow. Hundreds of workers were stranded inside the Bethlehem Steel plant, forcing many to desert open job stations and seek the nearest shelters. Crews manning high-wheeled payloaders and road-graders battled drifts and frostbite to rescue workers marooned at the ore pits and other distant areas.

Worse yet, melting snow running down the sides of the

coke ovens turned to ice as soon as it hit the car rails. With no traction, the cars could not move to deliver gas supplies; if air slipped into the unfilled gas lines, there would be a certain explosion. Disaster was averted only by alert workers who kept the lines filled by piping gas from the local utility directly into the plant.

Acts of heroism and dedication to duty in the seventy-two-hour crisis are today part of the lore of Lackawanna. Miraculously, not a life in the plant was lost. But the costs of crippled production, and emergency expenses in keeping the plant from shutting down, amounted to incalculable millions.

The next month, on February 7, an underground fire broke out in Bethlehem Steel's Cambria Division Coal Mine 32 in western Pennsylvania. Fires in deep underground mines defy even the most advanced fire-fighting techniques. The Cambria blaze proved particularly stubborn. Firemen failed to isolate the damage to Mine 32, and the blaze soon spread into Mine 33, which was connected by underground workings.

The mines burned out of control for several weeks, until finally crews managed to seal them off with special concrete bulkheads and then flooded the area. The sealing technique worked, but not without another heavy dollar-loss for Bethlehem Steel. Production at Mine 33 did not resume until two months later, and Mine 32 never did open during the remainder of the year. Not only did Bethlehem operations have to look elsewhere for bituminous coal, but the company lost considerable revenues in coal sales to other customers. Estimated costs incurred by the fire amounted to at least $15 million, not counting operating profits never regained.

However, the worst of 1977 was yet to come for Bethlehem Steel. During the early hours of July 20, torrential rains sent great sheets of water down the mountainsides surrounding Johnstown, home of a Bethlehem plant employing about twelve thousand workers. Small creeks became rivers, and the normally peaceful Conemaugh and Stonycreek rivers became raging monsters. Water spilled over their "flood-free banks" and flooded the city of Johnstown with currents so devastating that more than seventy lives were lost, and thousands were left homeless.

Rushing waters, laden with silt, ripped through the Bethlehem plant, shutting down virtually every operation and leaving a thick layer of muck after the flood receded. It took two months to restore full steelmaking again. The cleanup and restoration costs dealt Bethlehem Steel another catastrophic loss—an estimated $39 million—and some facilities could not be salvaged. One of these was the ferromanganese blast furnace that produced an alloy product sold to all corporate steelmaking shops as well as outside users.

The same flood also crippled three Bethlehem coal mines located in the Johnstown area. Mines 38-E and 78 were able to resume production in a few weeks. Mine 77, where machinery had been submerged under two hundred feet of water, was not operative until the following year. It cost at least $2 million to pump out the flood waters and restore operations.

As though all forces of catastrophe were conspiring to make 1977 a thoroughly snake-bitten year for Bethlehem Steel, in mid-December two huge supertankers owned by the company somehow collided in a remote shipping lane off the southern coast of Africa. Neither tanker knew the other was in the vicinity and apparently neither crew on watch saw the collison course on their radar screens. Two seamen were killed, and though oil cargoes in both vessels were contained, the accident put both tankers out of commission for eight months.

Never in its seventy-three-year history had there been a year as bad for Bethlehem Steel. The costly disasters could not have come at a worse time. Even without them the company's profitability already was being threatened for the first time since 1933, the last losing year. Earnings had steadily declined from $242 million in 1975 to $168 million in 1976, and a new wage contract signed in 1977 was accelerating the downward slide.

However, there was no indication that anyone had been looking at the historical sweep. As M. Colyer Crum, a Harvard Business School professor who sometimes uses Bethlehem Steel's decline as a case study in his classes, remarked in an interview, "They were in trouble long before. . . . If you have a board that basically pride themselves on their longevity and the purity of their association . . . you are basically getting yourself in a box where there is no cross-fertilization at all."

The wage agreement that replaced the contract expiring on July 31, 1977, extended the industrywide, no-strike pact to August 1983, but put a terrible strain on the balance sheet. By now a weakening market for domestic steel had made it virtually impossible to recoup the cost by raising prices. Yet the new agreement heaped on staggering new expenses. It granted two separate hourly wage increases of 20 cents each during 1977, and 10 cents each six months thereafter for the next two years. Worst of all, with inflation running at a double digit pace, were the punishing automatic increases under the cost of living clause.

It was obvious Bethlehem would have to close unprofitable and even marginal facilities to put its house in order. A prudent move would have been to view the flood disaster as a God-given opportunity to phase out the Johnstown plant, the oldest of Bethlehem's steelmaking facilities, tracing its founding to 1873. However, this was the plant where reigning Chairman Lewis Foy began his career in steel. And Johnstown's labor force always had been regarded as Bethlehem's most dedicated.

While the Johnstown plant had been rebuilt since it was acquired from Midvale Steel in 1923, changing times have been cruel to this landlocked facility. Steel markets were moving westward, and cheap rail transportation was a thing of the past. All materials had to be transported in and out at soaring costs. Hemmed in on one side by a river and another side by a town, the plant was landlocked in another sense. There was no room for it to grow. Putting new money into rebuilding a flood-devastated, aging facility was a poor investment, no matter how much sentiment there was to keep it going.

Similarly, there were good reasons to pull the plug at the Lackawanna plant, which traces its beginning to 1900. With the era of selling as much steel as could be produced ending, the older, less efficient plant could not compete with more modern facilities. For a time, Lackawanna had been kept busy by providing semifinished slabs for the new mills being built by Bethlehem at Burns Harbor. But now Burns Harbor was fully integrated, and its newly completed furnaces could turn out all the raw steel needed for its mills.

Further, Burns Harbor was situated in the midst of the country's thriving steel market, within the five-hundred-mile radius of Chicago that included all the major automobile plants. Each ton of steel sent from Lackawanna to Chicago cost $20 a ton extra for shipping, thus compounding the competitive disadvantages.

Finally, Lackawanna was a hostile plant town. Labor relations there created more problems than all other Bethlehem plants combined, and exploitive local governments made outrageous tax assessments to the point that Bethlehem was constantly turning to the courts for relief. There was strong sentiment within Bethlehem's headquarters to shut down steelmaking at Lackawanna before any reductions were made elsewhere.

When it became obvious that jobs at one or both cities would be lost, delegations of civic, political, and industrial leaders from Johnstown and Lackawanna descended upon Bethlehem to plead the case for keeping their plants in operation.

"I struggled with that thing for months," Lewis Foy says, "but I just knew there was no way we were going to cut it. So we decided to take a $750 million write-off, get rid of a lot of facilities, and a lot of people."

This decision was the largest write-off ever taken by any American firm. But instead of closing Johnstown or Lackawanna outright, Foy tried to divide the pain. The company closed the plate mill and several other older facilities at Johnstown, reducing steelmaking capacity from 1.8 million tons annually to 1.2 million. At Lackawanna, the company closed four blast furnaces, a basic oxygen vessel, and five rolling mills, among other facilities, cutting capacity there from 4.8 million tons annually to 2.8 million tons.

About 3,800 people lost their jobs at Johnstown as the total work force shrunk from its preflood 11,400 to 7,600. The reductions at Lackawanna brought employment down from 11,500 to 8,000. While those blue-collar cuts, announced in August of 1977, were expected—and even deemed merciful—it was not until the following month that near panic suddenly developed among the white-collar workers in the company.

An almost unnoticed paragraph in the announcement of curtailments at the two disaster-plagued plants stated that salaried and hourly employment and overhead would be reduced to "a level consistent with our reduced steelmaking capacity." But it was generally assumed that only personnel directly linked to Johnstown and Lackawanna support services would be cut, and in relatively modest numbers.

On September 30, 1977, a day engraved in the memory of Bethlehem Steel office workers as "Black Friday," dismissal notices went out to 2,500 white-collar workers across the company. Among the victims were 800 shocked employees in Bethlehem's Martin Tower and other headquarters facilities.

William Perry, a member of Bethlehem's media staff for six months, announced the terminations, including his own, to the press. As the newest member of the media staff, it was understandable that Perry go. The terminations involving low-seniority white-collar workers made sense. They were all support personnel, and their dismissal, as painful as it was, seemed consistent with the company goal.

However, when the body count of Black Friday was in, there were a number of victims whose terminations heightened the fears of job-security in Bethlehem's offices. Among those let go were such people as Robert T. Hayes, an engineer at the Homer Research Labs. Hayes, as well as his co-workers, was flabbergasted to learn that neither his exempt salaried status nor his twenty years of seniority was a protection against dismissal.

James L. Zoks, a computer specialist with twelve years' service, reacted to his notice by charging that Bethlehem Steel had disregarded its personnel guidelines and instead just handed department heads a "hatchet" to settle old scores. Many others who were let go echoed the complaint. These charges increased the concerns of those workers who survived the reduction in force, particularly those who were not on the best of terms with their bosses.

A glorious era was coming to a traumatic end at Bethlehem Steel. Over the years, the company had managed to keep the union from organizing white-collar workers with a simple strategy. It automatically passed along to them all raises and benefits won by the union with each new contract. Office workers endured none of the hardships of walking picket lines or even paying union dues. There were no layoffs during slack times and employees remained on the payroll even during work stoppages. Could there have been any greater security?

Almost overnight, the trust was shattered. Black Friday set off widespread suspicion that Bethlehem Steel would henceforth use layoffs, in the name of restoring profitability, to rid the company of whomever it pleased, particularly those who challenged authority.

Most vehemently certain of this supposition was Charles Vuksta, a thirty-year veteran engineer who often rubbed superiors the wrong way with his brusque manner.

Vuksta, an intense man who reads law books in his spare time, had a model background for success in the steel industry. His Austrian-Hungarian father, a bull of a man, spent a lifetime in the mill. Called "Tomahawk" by co-workers, he was remembered at No. 4 open hearth as a first helper who once tried to move fifteen hundred pounds of manganese in a wheelbarrow, a feat that would have succeeded had the wheelbarrow handles not collapsed. He retired with high praise for the company that, he said, rewarded hard work.

Young Vuksta followed his father at the mill, but fixed his sights on something better than a steady shift on the furnace floor. After working his way through Clemson University, he was recruited for the loop course, Bethlehem Steel's management training program.

Vuksta did finish the loop course but was assigned to duty in the ingot mold, a dirty, suffocating operation. After several other unsatisfactory assignments, he settled down in a job loosely defined as an efficiency expert. His mission was to report on wasteful work practices and inefficient use of materials. It was a form of snooping that didn't endear him to the men in the shops, and sometimes even to his superiors.

Vuksta claims he was the first to report how the men at the beam yard were beating the company's widely acclaimed incentive system. "Crews on the cold saws were paid for each structural section cut," he says. "Instead of cutting three or four at a time, they started gang cutting. They took maybe fifteen or twenty [structural shapes] and cut them in one shot. That's one cut, but they were paid for fifteen or twenty cuts."

Vuksta also tells of doing the first inventory of pneumatic tools. "They never knew how many air tools they had in the plant," he says. "I had them fill out sheets and found out we had four thousand air tools. I assigned each a works-account number and started to keep track of repairs. I found they used to spend three or four thousand dollars on a tool by sending it to repair shops until I pointed out they could buy the tool new for $250."

Vuksta reels off numerous more instances where he detected company money being squandered. However, he says, the plant bosses appeared more interested in maintaining harmony than attaining efficiency. "You can't imagine how often they told me, 'Why do you worry about it, we're making money.'"

However, Vuksta says, two additional developments made him a marked man in the company.

First, after being elected a councilman in the borough of Hellertown, adjacent to the Bethlehem Steel coke works, he opposed the company's support of a plan to build an interstate highway (I-78) with the least disruption to its facilities or its country clubs. Bethlehem Steel backed a highway route through the borough of Hellertown that would displace some ninety homes.

As councilman, Vuksta argued that no homes would have to be bulldozed if the route was moved farther north, through a portion of undeveloped Bethlehem Steel property. A delegation from Hellertown, led by Mayor John Williams and including Councilman Vuksta, carried the protest to the Pennsylvania Department of Transportation. They won their case. The homes were spared and a portion of Bethlehem Steel's property was ultimately used for the highway.

Subsequently, Vuksta once again put himself in the bad graces of the company. "Early in the Carter administration, the company gave us letters to sign protesting foreign imports," he says. "We were to read it, sign it, and send it to the president. I flipped mine over and wrote on the back: 'Mr. President, I have too much respect for you and the position of the presidency to send this as is. My actual feelings are that mismanagement and waste are bigger causes for the steel company's problems. . . .' "

Vuksta says what really got him into trouble was the gratuitous last line of the letter, where he wrote: "Being of ethnic background, I could be the best qualified engineer in the world and not succeed with this company." That comment compelled someone in President Carter's office to forward the letter to the Equal Opportunity Employment Commission, which regarded it as a complaint of discrimination against Bethlehem Steel.

Vuksta was fifty-three when he received his Black Friday termination. He felt he had an age discrimination case against

Bethlehem Steel, but he was in no position to incur legal expenses. Drawing up the papers himself, he filed a suit in federal court. The case was rejected in summary judgment on the technicality that it had not been filed in time. However, he appealed and did not give up until the Supreme Court in 1983 rejected his final petition.

Since then, Vuksta, who now works as a regional manager for a contractor's supply company, has been a regular dissident at the stockholder meetings of the Bethlehem Steel Corporation held annually in Wilmington. He takes a seat in the DuPont Hotel ballroom near John and Lewis Gilbert, the traveling dissenting minority stockholders, and usually outdoes them in berating Bethlehem Steel for mismanagement when shareowners are given the opportunity to speak.

If the human scars of 1977 are not easily calculable, not so the dollar damage. Bethlehem reported a net loss of $488.2 million for 1977. The report jarred the industrial and financial world and sent tremors into every steel plant community.

Aided by a brief national economic comeback after the recession, Chairman Foy managed to restore two profitable years—$225 million in 1978 and $275.7 million in 1979—before he retired as chairman. Apparently clinging to the expectation that new peak years were just around the corner, he made a bold but controversial gesture as his last hurrah.

At Bethlehem Steel's expense, he transported about 250 managers and their wives—nearly 500 in all—to a $150-a-night resort at Boca Raton, Florida, in appreciation for their help in pulling the company out of its 1977 doldrums and to introduce them to his successor, Donald Trautlein.

The celebrants played the resort's four eighteen-hole golf courses, fished the Florida waters, and patronized a free, never-closing bar, winding up with a banquet at the Boca Raton Country Club.

Foy and Trautlein were the banquet's principal speakers. Few in attendance can recall Foy's gracious amenities. However, the somber tones of Donald Trautlein expressing his determination to increase productivity, no matter how much it hurt, left the audience subdued. Obviously, Trautlein saw his job as propelling the company into a different orbit.

"Boy, are you in for a change," one wife remarked on leaving the banquet hall. "You're right," her shaken husband replied. "That was, indeed, the last supper."

Chapter 12

A DIFFERENT STYLE
AT THE TOP

ONALD H. Trautlein, an amiable, stocky, tennis-playing
accountant, may be the most unlikely person ever to have
head a major steel company. In 1980, when he succeeded
Lewis W. Foy as chairman and chief executive officer of
Bethlehem Steel, the incongruity of his appointment was
widely noted.

Trautlein, leaving a successful career with Price Waterhouse, was the first outsider to reach Bethlehem's top echelon
without being groomed in the steel company's elaborate internal management training system. He had neither made
steel, sold steel, nor even lived in a steelmaking environment
for any length of time, as had all six chief executives before
him in the company's seventy-six-year history. In fact, he had
been with Bethlehem only three years before becoming chairman—almost unheard of in an industry where leaders spent
decades climbing the corporate ladder.

Further, this unimposing, dry-witted raconteur simply

does not look as though he belongs in a rugged smokestack industry traditionally dominated by blunt men who find relaxation in driving golf balls 250 yards off the tee or sitting in freezing duck blinds, shotguns at the ready, to blast away at passing waterfowl.

The truth is that Trautlein was not the man originally picked to succeed Foy. Tradition at Bethlehem Steel gives a departing chief executive the courtesy to choose his top successors, and Trautlein was not even with the company when Stewart Cort, the fifth chairman, made his selections before retiring in 1974.

Cort promoted Foy, then president, to chairman and made Frederic W. West, Jr., a sales-oriented, former Cornell football player, the new president. West, tall and imposing, seemed to have all the right credentials to go to the top. It was taken for granted that he was next in line for the chairmanship.

However, Foy had to make some hard decisions as he faced retirement in 1980. No one could dispute Fred West's long record of achievement in Bethlehem sales, but Foy, still feeling the shock of Bethlehem's $448.2 million loss in 1977, sensed the company needed a complete change in direction. That change was certain to require more deep surgery within the company, and Foy began to doubt whether anyone on the executive ladder with years of old loyalties could perform the painful cuts with objectivity.

Trautlein had spent twenty-five years with Price Waterhouse and was a senior partner there when, in 1977, Foy recruited him as comptroller to modernize Bethlehem's accounting system. At the time, it was unlikely that Trautlein could tell a blast furnace from an open hearth, but he did have one significant strength. He had handled the Bethlehem Steel account during nearly all of his years at Price Waterhouse, and no one knew the company's fiscal condition any better.

Trautlein was with Bethlehem Steel barely eight months when he persuaded Foy, in the wake of the natural disasters in 1977, to close $750 million worth of aged facilities at Johnstown and Lackawanna. That helped restore Bethlehem to profitability by the next year. It also intensified Foy's respect for Trautlein's cost-conscious overview of the company. Before finishing his first year with Bethlehem, Trautlein was promoted to senior vice president and elected to the board of directors. That was the first clue that Foy might have doubts about the old line of succession.

On June 1, 1980, amid considerable unease, Trautlein, the man brought in presumably only to straighten out Bethlehem's accounting department, became boss of the entire corporation. He was named chairman without having been president, and Frederic West took early retirement soon thereafter. "We've got an unguided missile running Bethlehem Steel," I remember one middle-management employee remarking that day.

"I don't think that Lew Foy was satisfied with what was to be the normal order of progression," says Richard M. Smith, a vice president and veteran director of Bethlehem Steel, in defending Foy's break with tradition. "Over the years when we didn't have a lot of competition we grew pretty fat. That meant we were carrying people who were excess to our needs. As we started losing money, we realized we could not continue to carry that kind of overhead. We were in trouble. I think Trautlein was an excellent choice. He was not tied to the old ways."

Foy went to great lengths—some say embarrassingly so— to orient his successor. First, in early April of 1980 there was the Boca Raton spectacular. Then Foy and his wife, Marjorie, said farewell to the industry and community at a party at Saucon Valley Country Club, at the same time presenting Don Trautlein and his wife, Mary, to several hundred guests.

Finally, the Foys and the Trautleins embarked together on a globe-circling junket, visiting significant international steel operations along the way. Bethlehem's G-2 jet, with kitchen, bar, and seats for fourteen passengers, can easily circle the world, allowing for fuel stops. That worked out very well, enabling the travelers to touch down at such cities as Singapore, Cairo, and London.

Back in America, Trautlein settled down to grapple with reality. In his first report to employees, issued February 10, 1981, he addressed Bethlehem Steel's deteriorating condition with specifics franker and more alarming than ever presented before.

"Bethlehem started 1960 with total cash and securities amounting to several times its long-term debt," he said. "We had more than three dollars on hand for every dollar we owed. By the end of 1980, however, that situation had been turned upside down. Today we owe almost four times as much as we have on hand." This decline in fiscal health, he added, was rapidly eroding public confidence in the company. A share of Bethlehem Steel stock, which sold for $40 in 1960, was down to $26 by 1980, despite the company's capital expenditures of $7.5 billion during those two decades.

"Ladies and gentlemen," he declared. "Those facts lead to only one possible conclusion: Bethlehem is headed for even more serious problems unless we—you and I—do something to reverse that gloomy trend."

However, Trautlein at first appeared to be undermining his own message. Proxy statements mailed out to stockholders disclosed that he had increased executive salaries, including his own, as one of his first acts in office. Trautlein received $555,985 in 1981, his first full year as chairman. That was nearly double the $280,880 he was paid in 1980 when he was executive vice president.

News of the executive salary increases sent a roll of thunder through Van A. Bittner Hall, the headquarters of the United Steelworkers Union in Bethlehem. This was now early 1982, a time of deepening gloom for the industry, when two thousand workers were on layoff in the Bethlehem plant alone, and when steel company spokesmen were saying steelworkers would soon be asked to make wage and work-rule concessions.

About three hundred enraged steelworkers carrying picket signs marched on Martin Tower, the company's corporate headquarters. They made a few loops along the sidewalks in front of the building and then, amid cries of "the millionaires leave through the garage out the back," headed to the rear to block the executive exit.

No violence occurred, nothing much was disrupted, and the protesters disbanded peacefully after an hour. Trautlein later confided to friends that he was hurt by the demonstration. However, he doggedly defended the raises, insisting that the salaries now reflected a more honest compensation system for executives. Instead of hidden dividend payments, salaries were now in the form of immediate cash and in the open, he maintained.

Trautlein was born in Sandusky, Ohio, August 19, 1926, and grew up in nearby Bay Bridge, where his father worked as a watchman in a cement company. Young Trautlein served briefly in the navy during World War II, and then graduated from Miami University of Ohio. He won an internship at Price Waterhouse, and was subsequently hired by the accounting firm. Shortly after, he was assigned to the Bethlehem Steel account.

Whenever his work brought him to Bethlehem, Trautlein stayed at the University Club, which then offered accommodations only slightly better than a college dorm. In the city itself, where churches outnumber nightclubs by at least 25 to 1, solitary evenings can be quite dull. University Club regulars like Trautlein made it their business to keep track of eligible young women. Eventually, he was introduced to Mary Rankin, the daughter of a Bethlehem mining engineer. Today Mary Rankin is Mary Trautlein, and mother of their three grown children.

The Trautleins, who were married in Bethlehem at the Cathedral Church of the Nativity, an Episcopal parish, in 1956, raised their family in Darien, Connecticut, a New York bedroom community. When they returned to Bethlehem to live in 1977, they chose not to live in Bethlehem Steel's Saucon Valley executives' row. Instead, they bought a ninety-acre farm, about twenty miles away. Their home is an unpretentious eight-room stone farmhouse.

An admitted workaholic, Trautlein also raised a few eyebrows by removing Bethlehem Steel's main-office time clocks. Everyone from the chairman on down used the clocks to punch in and out since Eugene Grace installed them some fifty years earlier. "I don't want people to think their work is just 8 to 5," Trautlein explained.

It is a mark of the Trautlein style that he attacks everything he does with maximum vigor. However bad a start he might have had by raising the dollar amounts of executive salaries at the outset of his reign, he established quickly thereafter that he was a new breed of leader in the steel industry.

In June of 1982, three months after the union demonstration, Trautlein substantially cut his own pay and that of about two hundred and fifty Bethlehem Steel executives. Further, he announced there would be no bonus payments that year. His decision reduced compensation for top executives by as much as 28 percent, with no manager taking less than a 14 percent reduction.

With the salary issue diffused, Trautlein went to work on major business—an overall strategy to save Bethlehem Steel. Matters were worsening fast. After relatively modest profits during Trautlein's first two years—$121 million in 1980 and $210 million in 1981—the bottom began falling out for Bethlehem and for the rest of the industry in 1982. A losing year loomed. There would be no natural disasters to blame this time.

Trautlein recognized that a systematic dismantling of the nation's overbuilt and aging steel industry was inevitable. But all the companies traditionally had been reluctant to close facilities in which so much capital was invested, always believing a boom year was around the corner. Trautlein decided this was wasteful thinking; it was time to recognize the permanent changes in the industry.

His first priority was to convince his directors and managers that Bethlehem had to shed excess capacity—and soon. Speechwriter Jack Heinz observes: "Trautlein came along, slapped them on the cheek, threw cold water on them and said, 'Hey, you guys have been sitting waiting for a surge in demand for years and years. You can't afford to have all this standby capacity, in the sense of not only machinery in the mills but all those high-salaried people.' "

The white-collar overstaffing was apparent even to outsiders. As editor of the *Globe-Times*, I could not help but notice —and wince—that even after Bethlehem Steel's big bath in red ink in 1977, steel employees earning salaries higher than many of our news editors, were still used by the company as errand boys to deliver news releases to the newsroom.

"We had a rationalization job to do," Trautlein explained, when I interviewed him last year at Martin Tower.

The first attempt at "rationalization," which began while Lewis Foy was still chairman, had to be scrapped. "The people who were doing the study had been chosen from the inside. The result: they had a vested interest. Everybody was for their own thing."

To bring objectivity into the appraisal, Trautlein hired former Harvard business school professor Paul Marshall as a consultant and sought the services of a New York–based firm specializing in business reorganization. "We looked at each of our product groups and conducted studies as to how we stood with the competition and what was the outlook for the market: will it continue to grow or slip? We needed a framework in which to make investment [and retrenchment] decisions."

Trautlein also leaned heavily on the steelmaking sense of Walter F. Williams, a hard-driving engineer who moved up to president and chief operations officer in 1980. Williams made his mark with the company by supervising the construction of the billion-dollar Burns Harbor plant.

"We spent a year of long hours—besides running the day-to-day business—in trying to strategize, if you will, our company," Trautlein said. "And then we set out to do what had to be done."

The first thing to be done was to devise a method for reducing layers of excess salaried workers. Each work station had to pass a function analysis that had two principal tests: 1) Is what we are doing here cost-effective—can we do it with our own people or can we do it better by contracting with outsiders? and 2) With the company's declining capability in making and shipping steel—do we need this overhead?

A second major study was directed at streamlining the unwieldly corporate structure to make it easier to pinpoint responsibility. The years of empire-building without regard to efficiency were reason alone to justify such a study, but the erosion of workmanship made it mandatory.

In 1975, the Japanese had done the unthinkable by passing U.S. steelmakers in productivity. Now, in 1982, foreign steel producers were beating them on quality.

"We, the American steel industry, were not performing [up] to the quality standards that the rest of the world was starting to ship in," Walter Williams conceded in an interview. "We felt the impact first from our automotive and appliance customers, who told us that our steel was not up to their standards, and that if we didn't get it there we were in for serious problems."

The rejection rate of American steel reached as high as 8 percent, Williams said. Manufacturers complained much of it was inferior to steel from Japan or Europe because it didn't curve or weld as well, or because it just had too many defects.

Indeed, the Ford Motor company by 1982 had been rejecting and returning nearly 9 percent of the domestic steel it purchased. The "quality gap" became so troublesome that Ford and other American automobile manufacturers put suppliers on notice that they would lose the manufacturers' business unless they reduced deliveries of substandard steel to less than 3 percent.

Pinpointing responsibility for quality now took equal place with pinpointing responsibility for cost competitiveness in the Trautlein restructuring. Out of these considerations emerged a greatly decentralized company split into about two dozen business units that had to survive on their own.

Mining was split into separate divisions for coal and stone, for example, and steel operations divided into separate groups for bar, rod and wire, forgings, and steel manufacturing. Each had its own sales, accounting, and operating staffs. And each was accountable for its own performance.

Whereas an accountant in a Bethlehem Steel shipyard in Beaumont, Texas, once reported directly to the vice president of accounting in the headquarters offices in Bethlehem, he now reports to the general manager at Beaumont. Similarly, coal operations, fastener plants, and wire rope mills now have sales people solely responsible for their products. Nor does any operation look any longer to Bethlehem headquarters for labor relations help. The divisions are, in Walter William's words, "all a complete team, all masters of their own destiny working together to make their units profitable."

Unsurprisingly, the function studies and the restructuring showed that Bethlehem could operate with far fewer people, that complete departments could be obliterated, and that many services could be provided more cheaply by outside contractors.

The result, of course, was mass dismissals. Almost overnight, lives were changed, dreams demolished, and entire communities disrupted. Having designed a strategy to save the company, Trautlein now faced the test of whether he had the stomach to deal with the trauma.

Chapter 13

TAKING THE LUMPS AT BETHLEHEM

DURING every quarter, the directors of Bethlehem Steel walk down a gallery lined with pictures of their predecessors and convene to consider the health of the company and to distribute the quarterly dividend.

They meet in an imposing boardroom on the twenty-first floor of Martin Tower, taking their places in green leather chairs around a long oval table with squared ends. The two long-departed leaders, Charles Schwab and Eugene Grace, oversee the proceedings from their portraits, the only ones on the boardroom walls.

The board of this major American corporation represents power and exudes confidence. Once an exclusive club composed only of Bethlehem Steel officers, the board was diversified by then-chairman Edmund F. Martin in the mid-1960s. By the late 1970s, when the steel industry faced fateful decisions, Bethlehem Steel was drawing upon the talents of such outside directors as Ellmore C. Patterson, chairman of the executive committee, Morgan Guaranty Trust Company; Charles B. McCoy, chairman of finance, E. I. du Pont de Nemours & Company; William W. Scranton, former governor of Pennsylvania and former U.S. ambassador to the United Nations; and W. Deming Lewis, Rhodes scholar and president of Lehigh University.

Always seated in the boardroom, in chairs lined up against the wall, were Bethlehem Steel executives of varying responsibilities, and high-priced lawyers and accountants at the ready to brief the directors on any necessary details.

No one could be at these sessions without sensing the managerial majesty in the air. How could anyone entertain a thought that such capable, experienced executives could be incapable of dealing with the troubles that had been steadily descending on the company?

No one, perhaps, except Donald H. Trautlein. During his Price Waterhouse years, Trautlein attended board meetings but was among those on the sidelines, speaking only when asked a question. However, by the time he joined Bethlehem Steel, he must have known that the board was clinging to an unreal world.

Certainly, the board's delusion was glaringly apparent to Trautlein when he succeeded Lewis Foy as chairman. In a story on the transition of leadership, *Forbes* magazine reported that Bethlehem Steel's average return on capital over the past five years was a bare 3.3 percent, putting it next to the bottom among the majors players in the industry. Further, with at least $3 billion needed for modernization, the company's long-term debt already stood at an uncomfortable 28 percent of capitalization, and decreasing earnings were going largely into maintaining dividends.

With Trautlein's help, Foy had made a start at streamlining the company in 1977 by chopping off twenty-five hundred corporate jobs and shutting down some marginal steelmaking facilities. However, that only temporarily halted staff growth.

Within a year, the empty wings in the cruciform Martin Tower building began to fill up again, and so did the old General Office Building across the Lehigh River. By 1980, the staff was back in full force.

Bethlehem was nourishing a corporate bureaucracy headed on a self-destructing course. No one had really confronted the root cause for such undisciplined growth in the corporate offices: the internal politics of empire building.

When the vice president of finance and legal affairs retired, two separate vice presidents, with their own retinues, were named to replace him, one for legal affairs and the other for financial affairs. Similarly, when the vice president of industrial and public relations retired, two more vice presidents were named, one for industrial relations and the other for public affairs.

Steelmaking operations, once handled by a single vice president, expanded into a department of a senior vice president and two vice presidents. Sales, not be outdone, added its own extra set of vice presidents, followed soon by a similar expansion of accounting. In the space of twenty-five years leading up to 1980, the number of officers of vice president-rank or higher doubled. And each of these vice presidents required his own assistants, assistants-to, managers, assistant managers, and secretaries.

Further, the executives lived in a dream world of their own making. Each stratum of bureaucracy had its own status symbols: corner offices, lush carpeting, wooden doorknobs with corporate logos. No names or titles were on the office doors, but any Bethlehem employee could deduce by a quick glance at the decor in any office the managerial rank of the person inside.

Those executives lucky enough to make the long journey from a managerial job in a steel plant to a place on the corporate staff had to be astonished at the leisurely pace in the home office. Here there were no tonnage quotas to push. Most people in the corporate offices came in at 8 A.M. and left at the stroke of 5 P.M. Some higher-level managers came in late to avoid the traffic. They had no qualms about leaving at five.

Upper-level executives found copies of the *New York Times* and the *Wall Street Journal* on their desks when they came to work. Reading them commanded the highest priority during the first hours of the morning. The lower ranks brought in the local papers to catch up on the community news, ball scores, and race results before beginning their own labors.

L. Paul Lopresti, a company engineer, says he once grabbed and tore up a newspaper from a worker who spent the first few hours of each day doing the crossword puzzle, refusing to answer the office phone because he did not want to be disturbed.

The department supervisor called Lopresti into his office, and chided him for not respecting personal property. The puzzle fan, Lopresti says, had done the puzzle "for so long that it had become a past practice. The union had a written past-practice clause so the office workers just assumed they had one, too. No one in authority ever told them otherwise."

Even for those white-collar workers who took their work seriously, job fatigue at Bethlehem Steel was improbable. The company had a generous vacation plan. By 1980, workers in Bethlehem's executive suites were getting at least six weeks of annual vacation and seven weeks if they had twenty years of service.

White-collar workers also had twelve holidays to look forward to each year, including one to observe United Nations day and a floating holiday to celebrate anything. In all, the typical salaried worker at Bethlehem Steel received at least two months off each year with pay. Bethlehem Steel also permitted five days off in the event of the death of a parent, parent-in-law, wife, husband, child, son-in-law, or daughter-in-law.

The comfortable life lulled managers into being mere participants. Corporate headquarters was no place for risk takers. Salesmen weren't expected to sell. They became order takers. Promotions came from within. The system did not accommodate fresh views. When the good times were threatened and courageous decisions were needed, the company found itself with managers too paralyzed to make decisions and a board too loyal to the administrators to declare, "Bethlehem Steel is in trouble."

Such was the malaise Donald Trautlein inherited when he settled into the chairman's office. Before he could attack the excesses in the ailing steel plants, admittedly burdened by the highest wages and the most restrictive work rules in all of heavy industry, he had first to shake up and cull out the white-collar suites.

Trautlein began by ordering that the corporation's salaried staff of twenty-three thousand employees be reduced by 5 percent a year for four years.

For a brief while, it appeared that normal attrition would make the reductions painless. To speed up attrition, a supervisor, manager, or assistant vice president here and there was encouraged to retire a few years earlier than he had intended. The departures were amicable, usually enhanced by some form of extended severance. More than a thousand salaried people were phased out even before 1980 ended.

The next year, many employees were offered the option of departing with a lump-sum pension. This single-payment life-annuity was open to anyone at least fifty-five years old. If the retiree and his spouse passed the required physical test, the company paid a once-and-done pension settlement based on actuarial tables of life expectancy.

The settlements ranged from $200,000 for a veteran line foreman to as much as $2 million for a vice president. With interest rates at 15 percent in 1981, and rumors that the company might soon force retirements, thousands of employees and their families began to agonize over the option.

Oddly, until only two years before, the lump-sum payments had been allowed only for an exclusive few, former chairmen Stewart Cort and Lewis Foy among them, because the company had ruled a recipient had to prove he had "an amount of stable income from sources other than that which would be derived from the lump-sum payment."

The ostensible reason for this ruling was that the company wanted to protect the financial security of those employees who had no other resources to fall back on, in the event they squandered rather than invested their pension payment. But in practice it allowed only wealthy corporation executives to enjoy the lump-sum option.

A doctor at Bethlehem Steel's Johnstown plant is credited with demolishing the company's hypocrisy. His application for a lump-sum pension was turned down despite the fact that he could prove income from a private practice. His threatened court case is said to have helped persuade the company to open the option to all employees meeting the requirements.

Two other factors were believed to have been equally persuasive in discouraging Bethlehem from trying to protect the exclusivity of lump-sum settlements. First, the Internal Revenue Service was threatening to deny the company a tax exemption for such settlements unless they were open to all qualified employees. Second, with an estimated $2 billion in the pension pool, lump-sum payments suddenly were viewed by management as a handy tool to get rid of people without the payoff being charged to company operations.

Many salaried employees left comfortable jobs paying $40,000 to $80,000 a year because they sensed the deteriorating state of the industry. Others were privy to organization charts now being developed by outside consultants and saw their future vanishing before them. Then there was the aggressive sell of the investment advisors who besieged prospective retirees. Interest rates remained extraordinarily high and stock brokers offered a wide range of plans showing how it was possible to retire at age fifty-five and live in comfort for the rest of one's life.

Those who declined the option usually did so because they had mortgages to pay and children in college. But others simply feared the inactivity of retirement. Still others felt their services and position were indispensable. Finally, there were those who opted for the lump-sum but failed the physical tests, sometimes for reasons as demeaning as having doctors rule that a wife was too overweight.

This health test requirement was particularly galling. Both Stewart Cort and his wife had been in poor health when he retired in 1974 (with an estimated $4 million settlement), and both had died of cancer a few years later. Now, lesser employees were being denied lump-sum options because of mere obesity. (Lewis Foy, who had no health problems, is said to have received somewhat more than $4 million, plus the lifetime privilege to lease a company-owned house and estate bordering Saucon Valley Country Club. However, unlike the Corts, the Homers, and other high-ranking Bethlehem officials, the Foys have remained loyal citizens of Bethlehem upon retirement and are among the town's most generous philanthropists.)

The health of the entire steel industry continued to worsen in 1982. A troubled Trautlein escalated further cost-cutting measures. In July, he instituted a 5 percent across-the-board pay cut for the exempt salaried employees—those in middle- and lower-management who are not subject to wage and hour regulations. This followed by 15 days his order reducing his own pay and that of all 250 upper-level executives.

Then he suspended the cost-of-living adjustments for the office staff, the first time in Bethlehem's history that the company did not pass on wage gains won by the United Steelworkers Union to the white-collar workers.

The axe fell next on the company's liberal vacations and benefits. Out went the floating holiday and United Nations Day. Automatic across-the-board salary adjustments were eliminated; future raises would be based on merit reviews. Employees would be required to pay a higher deductible for the dental program, and company contributions to the employee savings plan would be reduced.

Finally, as operating losses continued, the modest goal of 5 percent yearly staff attrition was sharply increased. Trautlein upped the goal to a startling 20 percent cut of the salaried force by the end of 1983. A short time later, he got even tougher, ordering a 20 percent cut by the end of 1982.

The combination of pay cuts and accelerated job reductions shook Martin Tower as never before. The nudging of high-salaried people to accept retirement no longer was gentle. The public began to sense the magnitude of the shakeout when Richard Schubert, Bethlehem's forty-five-year-old president and vice chairman, announced in June 1982 that he was leaving and apparently had no new position to go to. Some months later he became president of the National Red Cross.

Trautlein's determination to shrink the corporate superstructure continued. The company's respected vice president of research, Dr. Donald Blickwede, chose a lump-sum pension and was not replaced. Vice President of Engineering Richard Hurd, deemed one of the most competent in the industry, also retired early and no successor was named.

Alarmed by the drain of talent, William Ritterhoff, a senior vice president, reportedly tried to persuade several of his managers to stay on. Three months later, an announcement of Ritterhoff's own early retirement was delivered to the *Globe-Times*.

By the fall of 1982, thirteen high-echelon executives had chosen to retire within the space of the year. Where once a retirement party for a senior officer used to be a special affair, with the officer's wife and family present, now as many as five vice presidents were lumped into a single retirement party.

The retirement rituals for senior people were, of course, small balm for careers suddenly terminated during the prime of life. The farewells were said and toasts were raised in the privacy of the well-appointed Weyhill Country Club, the adjunct to the Saucon Valley Club.

Trautlein, who had usually forced the retirement, was almost always a guest at the head table, although not always appreciated. "He had the nerve after reading my background in the brochure on the table to lean over and tell me, 'I didn't realize how talented you are,' " one forced retiree told me.

The elimination of a vice president often was followed by elimination or consolidation of his department. That meant his retinue of assistants and managers were next to go. The proliferation of "For Sale" signs in Saucon Valley and Bethlehem's other prime neighborhoods indicated that many executives and managers decided to leave the town behind them and head for a new sanctuary, usually a fenced-in condominum–golf course compound in Florida or Arizona.

However, distance was not likely to undo the trauma. Many left grieving, some could not even believe the terminations were happening, others could not bury their anger. "It was not leaving the company that hurt," one wife of a vice president with nearly thirty years of service explained. "It's how they did it. My husband still doesn't know where he failed or sinned. What can he do with the rest of his life?"

"Why have they done this to my husband?" another wife of a vice president in his late fifties asked. "They just destroyed him."

Trautlein never found a way to explain his actions to either the public or his employees. It is unclear whether this was a failure of his public relations staff or his own preoccupation with cost-cutting. Even ousted high-level colleagues complained they had trouble getting an exit interview with the chairman. Some bitterly charged that if Trautlein had had a real master plan to save the company he would have reached his reduction goals more swiftly and then worked to cauterize the damage.

Inevitably, the survivors, too, began to feel the anxiety. "I was prepared to give my all when I was hired by Bethlehem," one executive said. "I turned down many offers to [join] what I thought was a growing company. Now I hate to come to work. If I am not pink-slipped, someone I know probably will be. I hold my breath every day I arrive."

In an interview, Trautlein conceded to me he had underestimated the depth of the industry's problems. He did achieve his goal to reduce at least five thousand more salaried workers from the labor force in 1982. But they, too, would not be enough. Despite two years of mass dismissals, the remaking of Bethlehem Steel and the human anguish in the plant towns had just begun.

Chapter 14

DISMISSAL TRAUMA

No one could foretell the extent of the trauma as Chairman Donald Trautlein began to force thousands of workers out of their jobs in the downsizing of once-mighty Bethlehem Steel. Certainly not Jim Ross, an obscure worker in the company's human relations department, when he was called in by his boss, William Reusch, and told he was being assigned to a temporary project that shouldn't last too long.

Ross's assignment was to set up the first "outplacement office" for Bethlehem Steel. The word "outplacement" wasn't even in the dictionary at that time, but Ross, a management trainee who became an expert on affirmative action, needed no one to explain why Bethlehem might need such an office.

He remembered the anguish of Black Friday in 1977 when thousands of employees were abruptly cut from the payroll. Now new rumors of big layoffs were circulating. Some were saying that Trautlein's plan to restore profitability would result in employee reductions greater than anything seen before in the industry. Ross had to devise a way to buffer the shock.

While Ross was still setting up shop, the thought of dismissal was farthest from the mind of Steve Sinko, a top labor troubleshooter, on the fateful day he was called into the office of his boss and long-time friend, Anthony St. John, assistant vice president of Industrial Relations. Only a few months before, when demonstrators had marched on Martin Tower to protest executive pay increases, Sinko had received a similar summons. Then he was the man chosen to meet the protesters at the door.

Now it was August 1, 1983. This time Sinko, who was putting his son through law school, was called in and told he was being cut from the payroll.

"I left shaking," Sinko, then fifty-two, recalls. "I had just refinanced my house the year before and was facing $1,000-a-month mortgage payment. . . . Tony said there was nothing he could do. All of Labor Relations was being obliterated in the restructuring." (Less than two years later, amid continuing pressure of force reductions, St. John accepted an offer to join Chrysler's legal department, where he became vice president of Human Resources.)

Sinko, highly regarded as he was, was typical of many employees who were to lose their jobs in the new wave of retrenchments. The voluntary and forced retirements of 1981 and 1982 had not reduced the corporate overhead fast enough. And even eliminating seventy-three hundred workers by systematically closing down the entire Lackawanna operation during 1983 would not sufficiently stem the flow of red ink.

Trautlein now embarked on eliminating every position in the company that did not pass the stringent job-function and cost-effective tests. Not surprisingly, the studies showed that jobs had collected like barnacles since the boom years. With the inducement of lump-sum pensions now ended, the reduction of excess people in 1983 entered the brutal stage—outright dismissal, and no hefty exit payouts to soften the blow.

Industrial Relations was "obliterated," as Sinko had been

told, its functions eliminated as a headquarters operation and its responsibilities shifted to the decentralized groups in the field. Other headquarters services similarly were wiped out.

Trautlein decided, for example, that the company could make steel without chauffeurs waiting for assignments, all the while drawing a steelworker's wages; or without cafeteria workers, who received full-time pay and benefits, when temporary help could be hired and paid only for actual time worked. Eliminated also were Bethlehem's prize-winning photo department, its highly regarded advertising staff, and many lesser services such as newspaper clipping, banking, and travel.

Then Trautlein cut off the country club subsidies. Devious bookkeeping practices no longer would be required to make it appear that money paid for workers at Saucon Valley Country Club and the other plant-town clubs were legitimate payroll expenses for making steel. The only exception was for the exclusive Weyhill Club, which remained a subsidized refuge for high-level entertaining—and high-level retirements.

Grumbling country club members watched to see whether Trautlein would eliminate the company-paid security forces guarding executive homes, including his own. He did that, too.

Once the uprooting of unneeded services was over, the pruning turned upon the surviving departments. Each was ordered to slim down by a specified percentage. There were to be no more Black Fridays, massive dismissals followed by a return to normalcy. Instead, Trautlein insisted on "ongoing consolidation of functions." He wanted systematic, constant reappraisals to determine whether certain jobs could be combined or eliminated as steelmaking capacity was reduced.

Every manager was expected to achieve a goal for reductions. What followed in 1983 is remembered as the most dehumanizing era in the seventy-nine-year history of Bethlehem Steel.

Men and women designated as surplus baggage were

called into their manager's office and told that their services were no longer needed. Secretaries and file clerks, many with no more than a high school education, were abruptly discharged from jobs paying between $22,000 and $25,000 a year. Overnight, they were cast into the real world where the going rate in the Bethlehem area for similar skills was barely half that.

Having heard the sentence, a sobbing secretary would then be led from the manager's office to an adjoining room where Jim Ross and his outplacement staff were waiting. They stood by and consoled while the dismissed workers vented their emotions. More than a few became hysterical. Some refused to believe the dismissal was happening. Others kept crying, "Why me?" The counselors could only nod sympathetically, then drive distraught employees to their homes to help them break the news to their families.

Casualty reports spread through the company offices like bulletins from the battlefield:

• A secretary, suddenly summoned to her supervisor's office to be discharged, discovered that he had a doctor standing by because he feared she would require medical treatment.

• In a different precautionary move, a supervisor had a security guard stand by because he expected a violent reaction from a clerk he was about to discharge.

• An upper-level executive used a dismissal to exact personal revenge; he fired his sometimes rebellious finance manager at 9 A.M. and, within earshot of co-workers, ordered him to clear out his desk by noon.

Certain department heads went to great pains to avoid direct contact with dismissed employees. At Bethlehem's Homer Research Labs all workers were called to a meeting to hear that forced reductions would be made. While the meeting was in progress, an underling placed a letter on each individual's desk telling him whether or not he would be kept. Once they returned to their desks, the employees learned their fate. The human anguish was no less, but superiors were spared hearing those first cries of "Why me?"

There were no such headquarters refinements at the steel plants. When the company decided, for example, that it did not need all of its claim adjusters, four of the highest paid adjusters, making $32,000 to $38,000 a year, were chopped off with the laconic words, "You four are gone." So ended the steel careers of Bill Towne, thirty-one years service; Neal R. Snyder, thirty years; Luther Kemmerer, twenty-nine years; and Al Horvath, sixteen years.

Many of the dismissed workers contacted lawyers or spent hours reading state and federal discrimination regulations with the intention of suing the company for age discrimination. It was their misfortune to be the highest paid only because they were the oldest, many told themselves. Wasn't this a form of age discrimination prohibited by law? But none of the several dozen suits initiated after employee reductions ever succeeded; most were thrown out before coming to trial.

Not surprisingly, among those ex-employees searching the lawbooks was Lawrence Paul Lopresti, the engineer who made waves in his office by tearing up a fellow employee's crossword puzzle.

Lopresti received his pink slip at age thirty-nine, not because he was the highest paid and obviously not because he was the oldest. He believes he was forced out because of his zeal in his job.

The final straw occurred, he says, when he wrote a letter to Chairman Trautlein after a chance visit to the site of new construction at the slag dump. The dump is at a remote end of the Bethlehem plant, out of sight of the public and out of the path of internal traffic.

Lopresti noticed that a contractor was using imported steel from Britain to erect a $700,000 repair facility for the Bethlehem Mines, Stone, Slag and Lime Division. He protested this incongruity directly to the chairman, insisting that his letter was in the spirit of the company's own campaign of "Take It to the Top."

"I was disappointed to note that rolled steel sections used in this building were made by the British Steel Company in Great Britain," he wrote. "These shapes could have been rolled here at Bethlehem. This lack of commitment by Bethlehem to a Buy American policy puts us at a disadvantageous position in regard to our proposals for restricting imports."

The incident was leaked to the newspapers, purportedly by a union official. The British steel was torn out, and Lopresti felt that he had been vindicated. But that did not lessen the anger of his bosses for going over their heads, or that of the construction inspectors for intruding in their areas. Within a few weeks, he was informed his job was being eliminated.

Lopresti filed an action with the Pennsylvania Human Relations Commission. His case never reached a hearing stage. A fact finder ruled for the company.

Like many others, Lopresti admits his initial feeling of rage has been mollified by the company's outplacement assistance, which he has used to the hilt.

Eventually, the temporary project started by Jim Ross grew into a model of counseling. *Time* magazine even did a piece on it, crediting Bethlehem Steel in its issue of August 8, 1983, as "the first major U.S. corporation to develop a comprehensive program to deal with the emotional impact of permanent layoffs."

Outplacement assistance became a thriving business for Ross, who early on saw the need for a service to help distraught men and women to understand that life does not end with a dismissal notice. He soon resigned his human resources job at the company to form his own counseling agency, with Bethlehem Steel as his first client. Then his firm —and its chief customer—were acquired in a merger with Mainstream Access, Incorporated, a New York–based management-consulting firm.

With Ross as a partner, Mainstream Access obtained similar counseling contracts with other major steel companies. The original Bethlehem Steel outplacement program moved out of Martin Tower into a smart complex of offices in a new, privately owned office building on the outskirts of the city.

In October 1985, Ross estimated that Mainstream Access had counseled about fifteen thousand people dismissed from their jobs in the steel industry, seventy-five hundred from Bethlehem Steel alone. He found they had one problem in common: "[They] relied too much on the steel company, just as communities relied too much on steel when it was their major industry. We could not do much with them until we convinced them, 'Hey, you have to rely more on yourself.' "

The process of confidence building could not start until the terminated employee overcame "separation anxiety," as the counselors call it. The time for the pain to lessen was highly unpredictable because a firing sets off so many different forms of emotional turmoil.

One steelworker spent nine weeks in bed after getting his notice. Others turned to wife abuse, heavy drinking, and thoughts of suicide. Every plant town has a story of someone who took his life after losing his job.

"I have seen everything imaginable, from people throwing books at me to [going to someone's] home to help break the news to a wife who is a quadriplegic," Ross remarked in recounting his experiences. "One family of a dismissed worker brought a seven-year-old child to my office and asked me why she had stopped talking. Another guy [came] home from the Mayo Clinic after having his ear taken off on the job and put back on again, got his termination notice, and he's *still* cringing in pain."

Formal counseling for each dismissed employee under the Mainstream program lasts a week. It deals with options for career changes and assessment of abilities. Next come tips on the job search, how to write a resume, prepare for an interview, and how to use friends and relatives in networking for job opportunities. Secretarial help, use of the telephone, and access to dozens of trade and professional magazines with current job prospects are provided. After the week of briefing is over, a career counselor is assigned to each terminated employee to oversee his job-searching strategy.

This was Bethlehem Steel's gift to dismissed employees. Together with thirty days of extended pay and a termination allowance, which averaged about ten weeks of additional pay, the package was for some a decent assist toward picking up the pieces.

Most employees embraced the counseling services eagerly after the shocks of termination wore off. However, Ross said, some refused to shed their vindictiveness. "I've seen people who went out and bought foreign cars, people who said they would never buy anything in a can again, people who said they would write hate letters to Trautlein. It's energy in the wrong direction. We urge them to use that energy instead to get on with their lives."

The higher-level management executives, many of them accustomed to earning between $75,000 and $100,000 a year, frequently needed the most help, Ross found. They were most likely to get into what he refers to as the "losing syndrome."

"They lay awake at night wondering if they would still have their job had they done something differently," Ross said. "They feel, 'I lost my job, so there must be something wrong with me.' They are socially embarrassed to talk to friends because they no longer have a job. They keep thinking, 'I let my family down, I can't keep the kids in school any longer. I'm a loser at work, and I've become a loser in bed. I've become a loser everywhere.' "

Many of the top-level executives who were victims of the reductions at Bethlehem Steel were either the more mediocre performers or those who did not fit in with the new organization. They left defeated, with a mind-set that they would never find a job paying as much as they made at the company.

However, some made an amazing turnabout and eventually felt relieved at no longer having to conform to the Bethlehem culture. "The ones who found new jobs were those who became risk takers," Ross said. "When put in a new environment with different types of people, they discovered they could be comfortable with new ideas."

Ross concedes it has been particularly difficult for Bethlehem Steel secretaries and clerks, sales people, and researchers. Clerks accustomed to salaries in the $20,000 bracket find it painful to settle for less, and prospective employers fear they will not be efficient workers if they are hired at half their former pay. Sales personnel were never really trained to sell; they could satisfy the company just by being order-takers. Meanwhile, researchers are so specialized that there are few employers who can use their expertise.

The blue-collar workers required the least counseling. Because they were used to layoffs and planning for financial hardships, few needed the handholding. Ross found they were helped best by showing them ways to develop a new identity, which does not necessarily mean job retraining.

"The steel plant had been their identity in life," Ross said. "It is tough to get them to realize they are no longer millwrights or beam inspectors and that there is something more than working for steel."

Bethlehem Steel's total employment hit a peak of 115,000 in 1975. It stood at 83,800 when Trautlein took over in 1980. It was down to 48,500 by 1984. Ross estimated that 50 to 60 percent of the Bethlehem Steel employees dismissed in the Trautlein period found jobs within ninety days, but nearly all had to settle for less money.

More by necessity than by design, Trautlein's downsizing of Bethlehem did not stop in 1983, or 1984, or even 1985. The company kept losing money. Terminations remain a continuing fact, and this has thoroughly demoralized the company. The survivors work under the specter of fear, worrying when they will get the tap and whether they can readjust to the world outside. Further, the pattern of white-collar terminations in the latter stages of the slimming-down has caused many of Bethlehem's most competent people to wonder whether they want to stick it out.

"There are no marginal employees left now," one middle-management survivor remarked in one of my last visits to Bethlehem Steel. "They now are looking to where cuts can be made of higher-salaried employees, no matter how good they are. There is no longer a premium for doing a good job. You can be the company's best worker, but there is no peace of mind when you know that someone beneath you can do your job at a lower salary."

Chapter 15

HARD ROAD TO CONCESSIONARY BARGAINING

LLOYD McBride, a balding former union muscle man, had a square frame, arms the thickness of small tree trunks, and the eyes of a fierce competitor. At age sixty-one, he rose to the top of the United Steelworkers Union the hard way, beating Ed Sadlowski, a militant, street-smart challenger with a big Chicago constituency, in a bitter election for the international presidency in 1977. Then McBride embraced the Sadlowski dissidents and stood with them in a solid front when the slumping steel industry began to beg for contract concessions.

Because of this militancy, it was hard to believe McBride's words when, in November of 1982, he addressed company and union representatives in the sixtieth-floor conference room of the U.S. Steel Company building in Pittsburgh.

"Some people work hard and some worry," he said softly. "I worry." With a frankness totally uncharacteristic of any past negotiating posture, the tough boss of the nation's steelworkers admitted he was worried about the waning health of the American steel industry.

McBride's conciliatory message offered the first real hope for a break in the union's stubborn resistance to wage and benefit concessions. It could not have been a better tonic for the ailing industry. The collective losses for the American steel companies in 1982 were mounting at a pace that would exceed $3 billion by year's end. More than two hundred steel facilities had been shut down in the preceding eight years, permanently wiping out 200,000 jobs. The surviving steel plants were limping along at about 48 percent of capacity— the lowest since the Depression—and 140,000 workers were on layoff. Further, imported steel, streaming through the government's leaky trigger-price mechanism, was grabbing a record 26 percent of the domestic market.

The unyielding downturn was particularly ominous for Bethlehem Steel. The No. 2 steelmaker, Bethlehem was the least diversified in the industry and therefore the most vulnerable, losing $497.9 million in 1982. Chairman Donald Trautlein knew that even his drastic reductions in force would not stop the flow of red ink. There were only two other places left to look for help. One was the government, which had the power to curb imports of foreign steel. The other was the United Steelworkers Union, which held a labor contract that was strangling the companies.

Trautlein, who was preparing to lead the drive for protection from imports, was particularly sensitive to the need for labor's cooperation. How could the government be expected to help unless the industry demonstrated good faith in trying to heal itself? No administration was going to protect Big Steel against cheap imports, however important the industry was to the economy, when by 1982 steelworkers were making $26.12 an hour, nearly twice as much as the average manufacturing wage.

But concessions were not in the vocabulary of the United Steelworkers Union. Every USW officer—international, district, and local—is elected by popular vote of the rank and file.

And every steelworker election contest, whatever the level, inevitably boils down to deciding which candidate can be the toughest on management. Any candidate espousing concessions writes a certain ticket to defeat and invites a shunning at union hall. A stand for concessions in the USW demeans the memory of those courageous union brothers of the past.

The union easily dismissed industry appeals for concessions in the 1980 negotiations. However, in the spring of 1981, it again was forced to confront the issue. In a surprising development, the Canadian steel companies, which bargain with the same international steelworkers union as the American companies, dismissed past custom and balked at settling for an agreement similar to the one reached with the Americans. They held out for an hourly rate differential of $4 to $6 less than the United States contract. The USW struck, but the final Canadian settlement, when adjusted for the dollar exchange rate, was a victory for Canadian management. The new pact, giving the Canadian companies a substantial labor-cost advantage, sent a chilling message across the border.

Lloyd McBride promptly received a call from U.S. Steel's J. Bruce Johnston, chief negotiator for the American steel companies. "We don't have to look to Korea or Japan for threats to American steel," Johnston said. "The big threat now is Canada, right across the border, and that's your union doing it, Lloyd."

McBride acknowledged that Johnston had a point. However, nothing came of the protest until McBride contacted company negotiators early in 1982 for a meeting to settle the extension of ENA, the no-strike Experimental Negotiating Agreement. He was informed that the nine major steel companies covered by the basic agreement needed major concessions before any other matters could be considered. The recession had accelerated losses. It was urgent that steps be taken to renegotiate the current contract, although it had until July 31, 1983, to run.

In the meantime, the industry negotiators had commissioned an independent study of comparative steel costs. Johnston, who is executive vice president of U.S. Steel, said the results were as stunning to his own board as they were to the union. In the case of Canada, there was a wage differential up to $6 an hour. Moreover, the Canadians had a two-year capital recovery versus twelve years for the American industry, and also enjoyed a $30-a-ton tariff advantage.

Armed with that information, Johnston asked McBride to take back a message to the steelworkers. "We're the outfit that you've been dancing with for forty years," he said. "When times were good, this hand was never slow. We bought the drinks. We threw the party. Right now we're in deep trouble."

McBride took the independent study back to the full usw board. Next, on June 18, 1982, he convened the union's bargaining conference, which brings in union officers from all levels. The conference voted 263 to 79 to authorize the union leadership to begin discussion with the industry on economic matters. It was not a vote for a contract reopening, but was nevertheless the first union recognition that there was an economic problem.

Encouraged, the industry put on an intensive drive in the plant towns to convince the rank and file that the steel companies were in deep trouble. In July of 1982, every steelworker received a company letter with frank admissions about excesses in the industry never before conceded. Typical were these points in the letter sent out by Bethlehem:

—Over a thirty-year period, hourly employment costs have increased more rapidly in the steel industry than in every other major manufacturing industry, including petroleum refining, automotive, electrical, and chemical. Steelworkers are far and away the highest paid workers. And labor costs are almost 40 percent of total costs.

—Over the same period, productivity improvement has been worse in the steel industry than in every other major manufacturing industry. Higher steel industry wages have not been offset by increased productivity. In fact, when compared to petroleum refining, automotive, electrical, chemical and the average for all manufacturing industries, only in steel have inflation-adjusted employment cost increases been greater than the increase in productivity during the 1950–1980 period.

—The American steel industry no longer has a productivity advantage over two major international competitors—Japan and Canada. In fact, employment costs per ton in the American steel industry far surpass those of Japan and Canada.

—American steelworkers are the highest paid in the world, and the American steel industry pays a higher employment cost premium (the difference between steel employment cost and the average employment cost for all manufacturing industries) than do foreign steel industries. The steel industry cost premium has increased dramatically in the United States at the same time that it has been declining in all other countries.

Then, applying the contractual provisions under COLA, the automatic cost-of-living agreement in effect since 1973, Bethlehem estimated that steelworker wages would increase in the next eight years to $66.34 per hour. It stated that steel operations simply could not generate enough funds to afford those rates and still pay for the modernization projects that would permit the company to compete.

The letter did not particularly impress the officers of the USW. Negotiation sessions were held in July but an impasse quickly developed over COLA. The union wanted no part of a profit-sharing concept, proposed by the company, in which the cost-of-living increases would be tied in with returns from the marketplace.

The union said, in effect, tough luck. You didn't ask us for a reopening in good times. Why should we bail you out in bad times? And besides, the fat cats running the companies caused the problems, not us.

But while the union's solid front was saying one thing, McBride was having different thoughts. He knew in his heart that the entire steel industry was in trouble. He decided he had heard enough from the hard-line theorists whose advice sets policy for the union.

At the risk of a rebellion from the Sadlowski wing, McBride went before the international convention in Atlantic City in September, and openly urged the union to help the sinking steel industry. Surprisingly, he received nearly unanimous approval to reopen negotiations.

At the first gathering of union and industry negotiators two months later, a conciliatory McBride announced he still had reservations about the profit-sharing plan proposed by the industry. But, he said, the union would be willing to give up more than $3 an hour, with none of the money being restored until the contract expired in the summer of 1983.

George Moore, Bethlehem Steel's veteran labor negotiator, looked with raised eyebrows at U.S. Steel's Johnston. After nearly twenty-five years in the trenches, Moore almost could not believe what he was hearing.

McBride explained that his thoughts were to take $1.50 an hour off the current wage scale. That would lessen incentive payments by an additional 75 cents an hour. Reducing the Sunday premium rate from one-and-a-half time to one-and-a-quarter would yield 27 cents an hour. Delaying the cost-of-living raises until July 31, 1983, was worth 64.4 cents an hour; and a group of miscellaneous readjustments, including giving up two holidays, would bring the savings for the companies up to $3.42 an hour.

McBride's offer was a real breakthrough, even though industry negotiators continued to feel that steel could not survive without a basic—and permanent—change in the automatic cost-of-living adjustments.

During round two of its negotiations a few days later, both sides appeared to be heading into an impasse over COLA, but once again McBride took the initiative. After declaring a recess, he made a counteroffer: the union was willing to limit the cost-of-living provision to 25 percent of plant profits and no more than the actual cost of living. More importantly,

McBride agreed to no carryover of COLA beyond the final date of the contract.

Not unexpectedly, nailing down the final language in the agreement became a tense process. By the time talks reached a third meeting, McBride was clearly a troubled man. He was besieged on one side by his union colleagues who insisted he could never sell a $1.50 pay cut, among other concessions, to a union conference. He was caught on the other by Johnston and Moore insisting that their chief executives were saying they needed even more concessions from the union.

McBride, plagued by a personal history of circulatory problems, even thought of resigning, according to industry negotiators. However, he held on and a package acceptable to both sides was finally worked out.

At 9:30 A.M. on November 19, 1982, the agreement was presented for a ratification vote at a union conference in Pittsburgh. With rank and file pickets outside carrying signs protesting any concessions, McBride presided at a stormy session. After hours of loud and vociferous debate, the conference voted on the concession package. It was defeated 231 to 141.

"A difference of ninety votes," McBride lamented afterward. "If we could have turned around forty-six people we would have had it. But I don't know what else I could have done. I described the changed contract in affirmative terms. I responded to every argument encountered on the floor. I am sorely disappointed at the outcome."

It was the most devastating defeat in McBride's long career. He blamed three factors for his inability to sell the package to the union conference. First, he personally felt responsible for not doing more groundwork with the rank and file. Next, a flaw in the conference structure worked against him in that it permitted people who did not work for the coordinating steel companies to take part in the voting. Finally, he hated to admit it, but the membership was not as altruistic as he had credited them—they· did not like reaching into their pockets for 75 cents an hour, which was to be their share of increasing benefits for steelworkers on layoff. McBride resigned himself to not meeting with management again until the next summer. However, both the companies and the union were jolted by an unexpected announcement from Roger B. Smith, chairman of General Motors. On learning of the failure to renegotiate the steel contract, Smith warned that GM, the nation's largest automobile manufacturer, would start buying foreign steel if the union and the companies could not indicate by March of 1983 that there would be no strike when the steel contract ended.

The union attacked the GM letter as interference in internal steelworker affairs. However, as head of an international union, McBride regularly attended functions where he mixed with leaders from other industries. He knew the GM threat was a fact of life, as were the clamors from the nervous steel-warehousing people threatening to follow the motor company's example.

McBride brought the entire bargaining apparatus back into action. Industry negotiators were dubious.

"How many times do we have to sell this thing, Lloyd?" Johnston asked.

"You want to turn it into a three-ring circus again, having company tables, central committees, and all these people involved?" Moore moaned. "We are not going to change anything. If anything, we need more concessions. You've been offered a $29.95 dress. That's what it's going to be. You can put lace on it, but it ain't going to be worth any more."

A meeting to lay the ground rules for the new negotiations was held in January, but McBride was not there. He had suffered a heart attack that morning and was in the hospital. In his place was Joseph Odorich, the USW's salty sixty-seven-year-old vice president, whose main contribution, up to this point in the give-and-take, had been to tell earthy stories during recess.

Meanwhile, a rift in the steel company front suddenly posed another problem.

Twelve steel companies once had been in the coordinated

negotiating group. The number shrank to nine in the 1980 negotiations. Then Wheeling-Pittsburgh Steel dropped out when the company had to seek concessions from the union independently. Now, Allegheny Ludlum, one of the eight firms remaining, was pulling out of the group.

Richard P. Simmons, the feisty boss of Allegheny Ludlum, had long been unhappy about what his company was getting for its money. He had complained earlier that lawyers for the coordinated steel companies spent too much time in Washington pleading for import curbs on carbon steel, while forgetting the specific imports hurting Allegheny Ludlum, a major producer of stainless steel. Now, he felt the steelmakers' coordinating unit was tolerating "dirty pool"—to his company's detriment.

Simmons's gripe was with Jones and Laughlin, which had made an offer to purchase the failing Midland Steel Company, a stainless steel producer, on the condition that Midland receive substantial concessions in wages from the union. Since Allegheny Ludlum was tied into whatever the coordinating bargaining team produced, Simmons felt it was wrong for JL, also a coordinating unit member, to seek a better settlement for a facility that would be competing against Allegheny Ludlum.

Simmons's pullout reduced the Big Steel bargaining group to seven companies. Since Allegheny Ludlum was one of few companies making a profit, its absence altered the consortium's estimate of profit-sharing payments in place of COLA, weakening the committee's attempt to sell the union on tying in compensation to returns from the marketplace.

The sessions reconvened in February. Joseph Odorcich, his small brush of a mustache twitching, opened the meeting. "Lloyd [McBride] made a bunch of mistakes," he said, breaking into a sheepish smile that crinkled wrinkles on his bald head. "Lloyd's too good for this union. He don't understand the people. You know I'm street smart. I know the bastards. Lloyd should have gotten a mandate from them. He didn't.

I'm not going to make that mistake. This is going to be [done] Joe's way.

"First, we have to review everything from the beginning," Odorcich went on. "I can't sell anything I can't understand." Then he began to talk about minor local issues still to be resolved, saying that Bethlehem had about five hundred such matters, National four hundred, and so on. Later, he mentioned that union representatives from U.S. Steel were asking for a moratorium on plant closings.

"My God, you are going into business as usual," Moore protested. "This should be a review, it's not the 1965, 1968, or the 1971 contract negotiations."

"Don't get your pants wet, Moore," Odorcich said. "Trust old Joe."

Johnston and Moore fumed as Odorcich continued to raise still more local issues. They asked for a recess and went outside to confer. "We were so mad, we came back in and simply said there was no point to continue the meeting," Johnston said. "We told Joe, 'You've just backed away from everything we had in round two. You're piling more rocks on the wheelbarrow and now we can't get the wheelbarrow moving.' "

"Now gentlemen, calm down," Odorcich said. "We'll come in with an offer. Look, you don't have to convince me you need help, but this thing has to be packaged to look right. Don't you worry about these locals getting out of hand. I'm in charge here."

The company negotiators felt better—until the next morning. There was Odorcich in the newspaper saying, "Over my dead body will there be anything done to COLA." Johnston promptly notified Odorcich that he was calling his own press conference and would say, "This industry isn't going to settle for any contract that has a COLA in it."

Bitter exchanges set the tone for the next two weeks. Bargaining broke off, then resumed. Countless offers and counteroffers were shot down. Odorcich would back off with shouts of, "I can't sell what I can't understand." Johnston would accuse him of using that as an excuse for reneging on concessions previously agreed to. Meanwhile, McBride, who had the expertise and the sensitivity to bring about a consensus, was unable to lead. He remained in the hospital.

At 7:30 P.M. of an all-day session on February 27, the day before the deadline, both sides were far apart, notably on the revision of COLA. Both made impassioned pleas.

"The union has to remember that the industry has to stay alive and the union can't postpone taking on these issues indefinitely," Johnston said. "How is the industry ever going to get its costs in line if it can't do it this year? The union has a responsibility to do something meaningful in the way of reducing employment costs."

"I don't intend to be the presiding officer of the first major union in history that gives back COLA to an industry," Odorcich said. "I go out here a hero or a horse's ass. The best way to go out a hero is to turn it down. But I want to save the industry. What I'm telling you is I have to sell it to the workers."

The impasse was unbroken at midnight. Odorcich started to pick up his papers. "I guess there's no way we can get from here to there," he said.

Johnston and Moore adjourned to Johnston's office. "I guess the ball game is over one more time," Johnston said. "Three failures in a row."

However, just as they were about to leave, a heavy hand knocked on the door.

It was Joe Odorcich. "I came back with my last offer," he said. "No COLA the first year, 4 percent the second year, and 3 percent the third."

Four hours later, a final agreement was reached. At 4:30 A.M., Johnston and Moore boarded a helicopter on the rooftop of the U.S. Steel building and flew to the U.S. Steel hangar at the Pittsburgh airport where the chief executives of the steel companies were flying in to approve the contract. Odorcich summoned union delegates, who had been waiting all night, into an industry conference.

The first concessionary contract in the industry was finally passed by union delegates, 169 to 63, after a full year of maneuvering. The new contract was for forty-one months. The cut in wages was reduced from $1.50 an hour, which was rejected in November, to $1.25 an hour. All cuts were to be gradually restored before the end of the term of the contract on July 31, 1986. As Odorcich offered, COLA was suspended for the first year and reduced for the next two years, but it, too, would be restored at the end of the contract. The every-five-years, thirteen-week vacations were eliminated, and the union gave up a holiday, United Nations Day, reducing the paid holidays to ten.

The long-standing issue of work rules, which restrict the steel companies from making labor-saving changes, was never really addressed. The union did not yield an inch in the one area where the companies could have been helped the most. While even such laggard industries as newspaper publishing had by now given up crusty past practices, the steelworkers managed to protect them as inviolate.

So a multiplicity of high-paid craftsmen continued to feed on routine jobs that a single worker could perform cheaper and faster. With the industry in peril, an electrician, a motor repairman, and usually a laborer still had to be called in on a simple motor repair job, even if only a fan belt adjustment was needed. So jealously guarded was each worker's turf that a foreman was barred from making a routine adjustment to a machine even if it saved hours of time.

Ed Tkacik, fifty-two, who worked in the Bethlehem Steel tool shop for twenty-five years until it was closed, reflects bitterly on how individual greed became pervasive as union workers insisted on enforcing past practice rights to the limit.

"One windy day a sign is blown off the side of the building and falls in the driveway," Tkacik says. "The general foreman sees it in the road and picks it up. He brings it into the tool room to give to somebody to put back up. A laborer spots him carrying in the sign and files a grievance for four hours' pay. He gets it because here is management doing manual labor.

"We end up paying workers for not doing anything," Tkacik adds. "If you assign a man some place by accident, you might pull him back minutes later when you realize your mistake, but he gets paid the full day."

And if you don't correct your mistake promptly, the man becomes a permanent extra in the crew size, as other foremen have discovered. "One guy's sole function was to turn on the cooling sprays on a mill stand, and then turn them off at the end of the turn," an industrial relations executive recalls. "And that's all he did. He just sat there all day long. We found out that the job had come into existence because some years back a member of the mill crew had been injured so they gave him that job to keep him working during his recovery. However, when he got better, the job stayed. The union claimed it had become an established position in the mill under the past practice clause."

It was estimated that the concessions granted in the 1983 contract represented a 9 percent cut in wages and benefits. The companies projected savings of about $2 billion while the union gained an increase in supplemental benefit payments to its laid-off workers plus a promise from the companies to use all savings from the renegotiated contract to rebuild the industry.

Reporters asked a beaming Joe Odorcich how he intended to monitor the company pledge to reinvest the savings into modernizing the steel industry. "We have a research department that is as good as any in the country," he replied.

It was an unnecessary concern. The concessions did not restore profitability in the steel industry. The losses of $3.2 billion in 1982 were followed by losses of $3.6 billion in 1983 and $204 million in 1984. Profits did not return in 1985, and all indications are that when the contract expires in 1986 the industry will still be closing plants and still be in financial distress.

Lloyd McBride died on November 6, 1983, his death undoubtedly hastened by his hard fight to move the union from its gridlocked position on concessions. He was a courageous man. But the bullheaded resistance of the USW to even modest contract givebacks, in light of clear danger to the industry, continues to be a major problem.

The USW had an opportunity to show the country it could take the lead in a changing industrial era. Instead, it chose for the most part to stonewall.

Nevertheless, the modest concessions finally elicited from the union were sufficient for Trautlein to go to Washington with a clearer conscience. The hour had come to beseech the U.S. government to help the American steel industry.

Chapter 16

IN THE SUPER BOWL
OF TRADE LITIGATION

A seventy-five-foot steel beam with a painted message proclaiming "Stop Illegal Steel Imports!" sits on the parking lot at Van A. Bittner Hall, home of the union locals in Bethlehem. It is left over from a community rally in 1984 when labor and management at Bethlehem Steel joined together and launched a drive to persuade the government to curb imported steel.

There is really no reason to move the beam. The once-busy parking lot is nearly empty these days because so few steelworkers are working.

Many people in this country feel that burdening the nation with the consequences of import quotas to save the steel industry is illogical. For them, the beam is a handy way to make their point. That steel shaft costs about $900 if bought from an American mill. The same beam imported from any of several foreign steelmakers sells for $450 delivered on the dock in Philadelphia. Critics ask why American consumers should be deprived of that saving.

By 1984, nonetheless, Donald Trautlein was convinced that import curbs were a necessity. Without the endorsement or support of U.S. Steel, the nation's largest producer, he rallied other steel companies behind a well-coordinated push that forced President Reagan, a committed free trader, into a national showdown on protective quotas for the industry. This became an epic battle that the *Wall Street Journal* described as "The Super Bowl of Trade Litigation."

The deepening distress of his own company had persuaded Trautlein that the country could no longer put off confronting the worsening trade problem. Bethlehem Steel lost $163.5 million in 1983 despite massive staff reductions and hard-won union concessions. Trautlein believed that the health of his company—and indeed the industry—could never be restored without the help of government.

By the start of 1984, imported steel, much of it coming from government-owned producers in the Third World, had grabbed nearly 26 percent of the American market and locked the American steel industry into its deepest slump since the Depression. The domestic market was in complete disarray. Foreign steel was undercutting prices on virtually all commonly used products, sometimes to levels that could not have possibly covered their cost of production.

"It is difficult to imagine that for steel and many basic materials and manufacturing activities, this country has no stated federal policy or objectives, in a world where foreign countries are focusing on our markets and industries," a troubled Trautlein had previously told a House Subcommittee on International Economic Policy and Trade. He estimated that $40 billion in subsidies had been earmarked for foreign steel industries by their respective governments.

Up until now, the industry had relied for protection on voluntary restraint agreements and Fair Trade laws dating back to 1968. But these procedures were not working. Injured companies could file unfair trading cases but only on a one-product, one-country basis. Even when an American company proved its complaint, the guilty country could circumvent the process by replacing the controversial product with a slightly revised version and shipping it back under another name.

The Carter administration tried to help by instituting a trigger-price mechanism in 1978. This remedy was geared to the costs of Japanese steel, which set the so-called trigger price. When steel was sold below the price, it was regarded as subsidized and therefore in violation of trading agreements.

U.S. government enforcement of trigger-price violations was so unsatisfactory that U.S. Steel in March of 1980 filed its own dumping complaints under the old trade laws against European Community steel producers, causing the trigger-price mechanism to be suspended, since discontinuance of such suits had been a condition for the trigger-price agreement. When the government persuaded U.S. Steel to withdraw its petitions several months later, trigger prices were reinstated in a modified form, but they still failed to work. Steel companies continued to bring numerous unfair trade cases against a constant stream of violators. In a short time, enforcement of trigger-price violations became simply unmanageable.

While U.S. Steel had been the aggressor in bringing litigation in 1980, it did not, strangely enough, support Trautlein's efforts in 1984, to bring about import curbs. Fortunately for him, the United Steelworkers Union agreed to become a joint sponsor, thereby sharing some of the cost and providing important political muscle.

Trautlein reasoned that an industry-labor petition of injury filed under Section 201 of the Fair Trade Act was the swiftest way to force a reluctant administration to grant relief. The act required aggrieved manufacturers to prove in public hearings before the U.S. International Trade Commission, an independent agency, that unfairly priced imports were the most important cause of the industry's distress. If steel suc-

ceeded in proving its case—and Trautlein was certain it could
—the responsibility would then be on President Reagan to
accept or reject the ITC's recommendations for remedies,
which were likely to be either tariffs or quotas on foreign steel.

A compelling feature of this strategy was that the Fair
Trade Act required that the whole filing, hearing, and remedy
process be completed in eight months. If the industry won its
case with the ITC, President Reagan, who was running for a
second term, would then be forced to make a decision in the
fall of 1984, virtually on the eve of the presidential election.
A presidential candidate, even one with the most entrenched
free trade views, then would have to consider the consequences of alienating two hundred thousand unemployed
steelworkers so close to election day.

Smaller steel companies soon recognized the merits of this
approach and offered Trautlein their help. However, U.S.
Steel continued to balk, causing concern that the absence of
the largest steel company could doom the case. There was
speculation that U.S. Steel did not want to irritate the Reagan
administration at a time when its merger with Marathon Oil
was undergoing antitrust scrutiny. U.S. Steel's official explanation was that it did not want to upset the voluntary agreements to limit exports reached with Japan and the European
Community just two years previously.

Within the industry, U.S. Steel was insisting that steel's
interests would best be served by pressing for import-quota
legislation moving along in Congress, instead of seeking
remedies via the uncharted course proposed by Trautlein. "If
you're drowning, you grab anything that happens to float by,"
responded Trautlein.

Accordingly, on January 24, 1984, while an ice-and-sleet
storm glazed highways and closed airports, Bethlehem Steel
opened the industry's most massive import-curb offensive at
a press conference in the Hotel Bethlehem. With Lynn Williams, acting president of the United Steelworkers Union, at
his side, Trautlein announced that Bethlehem Steel and the
United Steelworkers Union of America had together filed a

petition seeking relief for the entire steel industry from imports under Section 201. The petition asked that the United States limit steel imports to 15 percent of U.S. consumption, the historical level of the 1970s, for a period of five years.

"There is absolutely no free trade in steel," Trautlein told the press conference. He said that international market mechanisms to temper abuses had broken down. Heavy subsidization and foreign-government ownership of steel mills had led to excess capacity and uneconomic pricing through the Free World. "Steel is so basic to the national security and industrial strength of this country that actions must be taken now to modernize and preserve the industry," he said. "Damages caused by dumped and subsidized imports are undermining [the industry's] very foundation."

International steelworker union president Williams, fifty-nine, who had been named by the executive board over Joe Odorcich for the temporary presidency of the USW, made much of the steelworker contract concessions. "Current employee sacrifices which will total over $3 billion should have put the steel companies in the black in 1983," he said. "Most of them are still operating at substantial losses because of the flood of Third World steel imports at subsidized prices. We are doing our part. The government must act promptly."

Despite the traveling conditions, about thirty media people, including representatives of national newspapers and magazines, covered the launching of steel's campaign to raise the national consciousness on the problem. So important did Trautlein deem the event that a company plane was sent to bring in out-of-town newspeople stranded by canceled flights. In a show of solidarity, a dozen United Steelworker officials, identified by gold buttons, were present and, along with company representatives, who wore blue buttons, answered questions while mingling with the media.

The first crucial test on the merits of the petition of injury occurred in Washington in May, at public hearings convened by the International Trade Commission. By now the fight had attracted so much interest that the proceedings had to be moved from the modest trade commission conference room into the Commerce Department auditorium, which seats more than three hundred people. Before the bright lights of TV cameras and the presence of the nation's press, the story of an industry reeling toward insolvency because of "supply-pushing" foreign producers unfolded in terms that would have won the envy of any malpractice lawyer.

While a 201 petition is essentially a legal proceeding, Trautlein was not content to leave his case in the hands of lawyers alone. Led by Curtis H. Barnette, vice president and general counsel who was Trautlein's chief legal strategist, nearly the entire top management of Bethlehem Steel took part in detailing the scope of injury.

Bethlehem Steel President Walter F. Williams said imports were the largest factor in his company's profit shortfall. He said Bethlehem lost $1.25 billion between 1977 and 1983 and estimated that its lost revenues attributable to imports for just the four years of 1979–1983 amounted to $1.9 billion. He said Bethlehem's five-year modernization program, started in 1981, was in jeopardy.

"It is my personal opinion," Vice President of Finance Robert C. Wilkins predicted grimly, "that within three years the steel industry will not exist as it is presently constituted. Those major integrated steel companies not in some form of reorganization or bankruptcy will be owned or effectively controlled by the U.S. government as the result of a massive bailout program or they will be owned by one of the foreign steel companies which participated in the destruction of a proud industry."

When it was labor's turn, USW President Williams, gaunt and bespectacled, was fully as eloquent, reminding the commission that steelworkers did their share by taking a pay cut in 1983.

Then there were the analysts, lawyers, and experts hired by Bethlehem Steel at hefty fees to back up all that industry and the union claimed. Consultant Paul W. Marshall declared that "Very conservative analyses show that over the 1977–

1983 period employment injury has averaged a minimum of about ten thousand jobs lost per year, rising to seventeen thousand jobs in the peak import year of 1982. This injury translated into a loss of $2.4 billion in direct steelworker compensation alone over the 1977–1983 period." Marshall added that the total loss to the country was much greater because of the multiplier effect on other employment sections, on tax revenues, and on increased government benefit payments.

In spite of this *blitzkrieg* of carefully orchestrated and seemingly documented peril, the steel industry won its case only by a three to two vote of the International Trade Commission, its members so divided that they prolonged the debate after the voting was over. "The steel industry generally is seriously injured," insisted Albert E. Eckes, Jr., a Reagan appointee from Ohio State University, speaking for the majority. "Imports do not come close to being the most important problem," countered Paula Stern, a Tennesseean appointed by President Carter. "Number one [cause] is the general decline in demand." Susan Liebeler, a Reagan appointee who was the other dissenter, deplored the high wages paid American steelworkers; she felt any protection for the industry should contain a requirement that workers take a 20 percent pay cut.

The ITC determined that protection should be extended to five major steel products. Although the industry had asked protection for nine, the five products represented 70 percent of steel imports in 1983. They included sheets and strips used in appliances and cars, plates used in bridges and ships, and structural shapes, wire rods, and semifinished steel used in construction.

The significant trade victory surprised the skeptics and catapulted Trautlein, little known only three years earlier, into a clear leadership role in the industry. However, there was yet the danger that the ruling's significance could vanish as fast as it occurred. The finding was one of injury. It was meaningless unless the petitioners were granted the right remedies to deal with the injury.

In the Super Bowl of Trade Litigation

The International Trade Commission reconvened in June to determine what remedies it would recommend to President Reagan. With the most stringent trade curbs in modern times now a possibility, the hearings received even wider international attention. Thirteen separate television teams, including those from foreign nations like France and Japan, reported the proceedings.

Once more, Bethlehem's Trautlein headed the parade of witnesses from industry, labor, government, and the independent sector. By now, U.S. Steel was publicly throwing its full weight behind Trautlein's appeal "that no remedy other than quotas will solve the very serious injury that has been suffered by the domestic producers."

Predictably, Fred Lamesch, president of the American Institute for Imported Steel, which represents seventy steel importers, vigorously opposed quotas as counterproductive. However, a number of government agencies also registered impressive protests. The Congressional Budget Office projected billions of dollars in costs to consumers and taxpayers and predicted import quotas would cost jobs in industries using steel.

Amid the deluge of pro and con statistics, the greatest impact was probably made by a surprise ally, the blunt Felix G. Rohatyn, an investment banker who is best known for his role in engineering the bailout of New York City when it teetered on bankruptcy. For a while, observers might have wondered whose side he was on. Rohatyn blamed the domestic steel industry for contributing greatly to its own problems, charging that "obsolete plants, insufficient and imprudent investment, weak management and high labor costs" all played a part in the decline of the companies. Further, he predicted that steel import quotas would be sure to raise steel prices and intensify international banking problems by making it more difficult for developing nations to find the revenue to repay their huge debts.

Having given good reasons to deny quotas, Rohatyn then urged the ITC to give the ailing companies one more chance to pull themselves together by providing the "breathing space" they needed to modernize and become more competitive. "Grant the relief the industry is seeking," he said. "If our steel industry cannot reform itself within the proposed five-year period, we probably should give it up."

On July 12, barely three weeks after the hearings ended, the International Trade Commission, again split by a vote of 3 to 2, recommended that President Reagan give broad new protections for the steel industry. It essentially backed the industry's request for a five-year schedule of relief. The commissioners added the condition that the U.S. industry modernize its plants, improve its management practices, and adopt major cost-cutting measures.

The ball was now in President Reagan's yard. He could accept the recommendations, substitute his own remedies, or reject any form of relief. However, the law required that he act by September 24, six weeks before the election.

For the next two months, the White House was deluged with thousands of letters—many in the forms provided by Bethlehem Steel—from steel employees and supporters urging quotas on foreign steel. A different mood came over the plant towns. Steelworkers decorated their cars with bumper stickers proclaiming "Foreign Steel Steals Jobs" and "Out of Work? Eat Your Toyota." They raised clenched fists at Honda and Toyota drivers stopped at traffic lights.

Meanwhile, pressures came with similar intensity from the opposition. European steelmakers warned that accepting the ITC recommendations could not only prompt the European Community to abrogate the 1982 trading treaty, but could set off retaliatory action against U.S. imports.

Outcries across the land likened protection for steel to the infamous Smoot-Hawley Tariff of 1929, which, many economists contend, inspired retaliation from abroad and hastened the Depression. Steel economist Robert Crandall of the Brookings Institution called quotas a "prescription for disaster," claiming they would insulate steel from competition.

Newspapers ranging from the *New York Times* to the Bethlehem *Globe-Times* argued against the quotas in language that said, essentially, that special-interest protection even for an industry as beleaguered as steel violated the public interest.

Reagan, who kept reiterating his commitment to free trade, had more than ample philosophical support to stand on his conviction. However, there was more to consider. This was impressed upon him by a delegation of eight Republican senators and fourteen Republican representatives from the congressional steel caucus who visited him in September, only days before he had to make his decision.

Representative Don Ritter of Bethlehem, a onetime free trader who was now championing quotas, explained what took place: "Each House member spoke from the perspective of his district. Dick Schulze, who had been on the defense committee, spoke about national security. Others spoke of the effect on people, the human costs. Each had a case to make." Senator John Heinz of Pennsylvania led his colleagues through a similar round robin.

On September 18, a week before the deadline, President Reagan announced his decision. He said he would immediately impose a plan to limit steel imports by negotiating agreements with all steel-producing nations. While studiously avoiding references to quotas, he said the plan would limit imports for five years to 18.5 percent of U.S. consumption. The White House emphasized these were voluntary restraints, in no way violating the principles of free trade. But it was clear that the plan was a protectionist action, worded in a masterly fashion.

Meanwhile, the jury will be out for several years on the full impact of Trautlein's campaign to help the industry. The administration did negotiate voluntary restraint agreements with fifteen countries, including such Third World price-cutters as South Korea, Brazil, and Mexico. However, there were no agreements with Canada, Argentina, or Sweden, and England delayed the signing of quota pacts with the European

Community to the end of 1985 by holding out for increased steel shipments to an Alabama plant in which a British firm has a minority interest.

Nor did imports slow significantly a year later. Up to October 1985, they were still running at about 25 percent—far from the 18.5 percent goal set by Reagan. While there were signs of deceleration, there was also growing evidence of circumvention. Some countries cut down on shipments of unfinished steel products covered by quotas, while exporting more products processed just enough to escape classification.

A second area of concern was circumvention through nontraditional suppliers. For example, one steelmaker complained that Panama, which has no mill and is therefore not covered by quotas, suddenly began sending in shiploads of steel. Obviously, a steel-producing country was using Panama as a conduit for exports that quota agreements would have stopped.

After a year's experience with import restraints, it is clear they are not a panacea. Quotas may help, but they are no substitute for enlightened management and labor practices.

Yet, as the distress in once-vibrant steel towns grows, another factor in determining the health of the industry keeps surfacing. This is the steel community. A town's civic and business climate contributes to the steel decline or helps halt it, as I learned in a trip across eastern America's Rust Belt.

Chapter 17

AFTER THE PLANT SHUTS DOWN

T was early November 1984, but I could already feel the chill of winter in the breeze off Lake Erie as I walked into the 8 A.M. mass at the Queen of All Saints Church in Lackawanna. The church, which fronts on Ridge Road and extends to a slag heap in the rear, serves the First Ward neighborhood that grew up next to the once-bustling Bethlehem mill.

Only two elderly people were in church that Thursday morning. With the resigned frustration of an inner-city clergyman, the Reverend Ronald Lord, a pleasant, middle-aged priest, bowed and blessed the congregation as though he had a full house.

Two blocks away, on a littered lot down from the corner liquor store on Steelawanna Avenue, another morning ritual was drawing a little better. About a half dozen men, most of them ex-steelworkers, one passing a bottle wrapped in a brown paper bag, were waiting, as they said they do each morning, for someone to drive up and offer them a day's work.

Lackawanna is a city without a pulse. It was severely stricken in October 1983 when Bethlehem Steel all but stopped steelmaking in this one-industry town. An estimated 7,300 well-paying jobs in this city of 21,700 people disappeared and the ripple effect took many other jobs with them in one of the largest single industrial shutdowns in the nation.

Three generations of Lackawanna families had poured steel for a cross section of American industry since 1900. Bethlehem Steel acquired Lackawanna Iron and Steel in 1922, and by the 1960s expanded the annual steelmaking capacity there to more than 5,720,000 net tons. Lackawanna became the third largest steel producer in the world with a work force of 21,000. Company brochures say the annual payroll during the peak years reached $120 million.

Today, the plant lies ghostlike on the shores of Lake Erie. It is an industrial corpse, a cannibalized complex of lifeless smokestacks, black buildings, motionless booms, and empty rails. The only sign of life is at the far end, where plumes of steam rise from the coke works. Only a bar mill and the galvanizing and cold strip mills across Highway 5 still turn out steel products, from semifinished steel shipped in from Johnstown and Burns Harbor. The plant's total work force is down to 1,300 and rumors abound that it may soon shrink more.

The public and private job-training programs, federal and state subsidized lifelines, and accelerated plans for industrial development have not significantly eased Lackawanna's deep distress. It is today the foremost single casualty of the American steel industry. Visiting the city late in 1984—one year after the shutdown—I could sense trauma everywhere.

"The loss of the Bethlehem plant has taken away hope," Father Lord said, sitting down to a cup of coffee after shedding his vestments. "It's not the church I worry about. I feel for the men in their forties and fifties. They thought they had secure jobs for life. And our young [people] now either have to move out of town or give up their hopes of finding jobs."

"There's no money coming in," complained two ex-steel-workers, who gave their names as Bill Rodgers, thirty-five, and Bill Myers, also thirty-five, when I stopped at the outdoor "unemployment lot" at Steelawanna Avenue. Rodgers said he had worked in the blast furnace but was several years short of qualifying for a pension. He had entered the federal retraining program and for a while held a job driving a school bus at minimum wage. Both men said they were separated from their families, and both claimed not to know the whereabouts of wives or children. Each said he was barely coping, with the help of welfare and the few dollars earned when a construction or cleanup truck rolled up to hire an extra hand.

Impressions didn't improve as I walked down Ridge Road to "the better side of the tracks." I found gloomy people shuffling along the sidewalks, sometimes peering listlessly into store fronts and sometimes stopping to chat with others about their setbacks. "For Sale" signs obscured the shrubbery in front of homes in nearly every block. At the town library, a clerk, busy checking out books, urged me not to leave without signing a petition to protest the threat to close their library because of Erie County's $75 million budget shortfall.

"We lost about $4.1 million a year in real estate taxes," said Lackawanna Mayor Thomas E. Radich, himself a displaced steelworker. "For years we depended on this one industry. When it went, we had to live with less. Thirty-five people were laid off in public works . . . twelve jobs were eliminated in the police department . . . eight in the fire department. People are moving out of town because they can't find work."

Nowhere was gloom thicker than at 650 Ridge Road, the site of union hall. A huge "For Sale" sign was posted in front when I visited this headquarters building. It once teemed with dues-paying members from four locals, but the shutdown wiped out one local entirely and reduced membership in the other three by a startling 95 percent.

No one was manning the front desk when I walked in. The only voices came from the second floor where I found Arthur

Sambuchi, president of Local 2603, sitting behind his desk and talking with Tom McMasters, chief grievance officer, and Wiley Cole, treasurer.

They were in mourning on this fall day because of the defeat of Democrat Walter Mondale. Sambuchi said that the steelworkers had worked hard to turn out Erie County for Mondale, one of the few New York counties he won. He and his fellow officers in the local went bowling to celebrate after the polls closed, but were crestfallen when they saw the Reagan vote roll in nationally.

Sambuchi, a slender man in his forties, has a firebrand personality and the reputation of being one of the toughest presidents in the United Steelworkers Union. He voted against contract concessions to the end, and virtually snarls at the mention of the Bethlehem Steel shutdown. He insists that padded management and corporate bias against the Lackawanna plant brought about its demise.

Sambuchi became compassionate only when he was asked how his fellow workers have reshaped their lives since the shutdown.

"Our membership is dying off, getting divorced, scraping jobs wherever they can find them," he said. "One worker was found hanging [from a beam] at his home after his job ended." He reeled off other tragedies, including the case of a laid-off steelworker who was two years short of a pension and saddled with family medical expenses. Sambuchi said the worker suffered the indignity of having the gas in his home turned off on the day his child died of leukemia.

"There is a lot of tragedy," Cole added. "What the hell, even I have a close relative who had to go on welfare when his job ended. Now his wife is leaving him."

The union reported that only about eleven hundred of the seventy-three hundred discharged workers qualified for pensions, which range from about $900 to $1,200 a month. The rest, mostly younger employees, were exhausting their unemployment compensation and supplementary benefits.

Many unpensioned steelworkers swallowed their pride

and applied for welfare, virtually swamping the Erie County public assistance office. "In 1980, we had twenty-three thousand cases," said Robert Ranke, deputy commissioner of social services in Erie County. "When Bethlehem Steel started mass layoffs, home relief cases and aid to dependent children skyrocketed, reaching a high of thirty-eight thousand last April."

A yellowed clipping posted on the bulletin board at union hall reported that Erie County Partnership, a private industry council, had opened an office for job retraining at 609 Ridge Road, only a block away from USW headquarters.

Asked whether the partnership was helping displaced steelworkers, Sambuchi shook his head. "Nobody calls us," he said. "There is no agency that calls and says, 'Can we help?'"

I walked down to 609 Ridge Road, intending to ask what was hindering the retraining, but a stern though polite woman would answer no questions. She insisted I go to Buffalo and direct my inquiries to her boss, Peter Russ, director of operations for the Erie County Partnership.

When I did see Russ, a former Buffalo newspaperman, he told me that Erie County Partnership had succeeded the Comprehensive Employment Training Act (CETA), the government retraining program for the unemployed. Under Title 3 funds, he said, the partnership could offer on-the-job training with 50 percent of the wages subsidized by government. However, he admitted the program has not done much for ex-steelworkers.

Steelworkers resist retraining for jobs that pay less than half the money they have been used to, he said. "Furthermore," he added, "employers are scared of steelworkers.

"We call up and say we have people qualified for the job orders that they want," Russ continued. "And they tell me, 'Don't send me a steelworker.' I say, 'Well, why don't you see the man and talk to him?' And they say, 'I don't want to see them . . . poor work habits. When they were working, they got everything they asked for. I don't need that.'"

His office was finding it difficult, Russ said, to offset the steelworker image: "That they got big dollars, great benefits, and the big thing was to get into a corner and go to sleep."

Fewer than fifty steelworkers applied for retraining with his agency. "And so the welfare load has zoomed out of sight."

The spacious parking lots that surround the office tower complex that used to be Bethlehem Steel's Lackawanna headquarters were empty. All entrances were locked except at a far wing where pension claims were still handled. The caretaker operations were conducted from a small, soot-stained building down Highway 5, across the street from the idle plant.

R. W. Caldwell, Jr., a young executive trained as a grievance officer, ran the office with the title of superintendent, administrative services. He presented a formal front, but intense emotions surfaced when the conversation turned to the closing of the Lackawanna plant and what might have been.

Concerns about the future of the facility first started when Bethlehem built its new, integrated steel facility at Burns Harbor in the 1960s. Anxieties heightened as imports increased and competition from nonunion minimills started to hurt. Bethlehem, like other major producers, found itself looking for ways to cut overcapacity.

"We in Lackawanna felt we were in competition with Johnstown for survival," Caldwell said. "We thought we had the better plant, a more efficient operating plant, more experience metallurgically . . . and the newest bar mill in the industry."

But Caldwell admitted he was not surprised when he was called in from vacation, in late December of 1982, for an emergency meeting of all superintendents in the general manager's conference room. There he and his colleagues learned the bad news.

Many considerations were cited, Caldwell said. Bethlehem had lost more than $100 million at Lackawanna in 1981. Markets had shifted westward and could be served better by Burns Harbor. Accessibility to the Great Lakes and St. Lawrence Seaway no longer was the advantage it used to be. The investment to replace old facilities, particularly the hot mill, was deemed too formidable.

However, many believed that the ancient, cramped, and flood-ravaged plant at Johnstown had all those disadvantages and more. Clearly Bethlehem's decision had been influenced also by other considerations.

Indeed, Chairman Donald Trautlein's announcement of the shutdown strongly suggested that the city of Lackawanna had been gouging the company on taxes. Taxes at Lackawanna had been more than five times the average amount paid per ton of shipments at Bethlehem's five other major steel plants, he stated.

Donald E. Stinner, a tax comptroller at Bethlehem headquarters, said the records showed the plant twice had been subjected to arbitrary property tax assessment increases—an $8 million jump one year and $17 million in another—with no real recourse or consideration of depressed business conditions. Since Bethlehem used to pay 73 percent of the property taxes in Lackawanna, it was easy to see how socking it to the steel company became an easy way for inefficient city administrations to cover their sins.

Caldwell, the caretaker officer, recalled that the company even sent fiscal experts to advise the city on how to put its municipal affairs in shape. When their recommendations were ignored, Bethlehem sued the city over its tax bills for five consecutive years starting in 1978. Each such action seemed to be met with the attitude, "What are you going to do about it? You have too much of an investment to pull out."

After Bethlehem shut down the plant, Lackawanna conceded the inequity. All legal actions were settled out of court and Bethlehem's tax bills were cut retroactively, from $13.5 million in 1982 to 9.5 million in 1983, and to $6 million in 1984. In 1985, taxes were expected to be $2.5 million.

While Bethlehem Steel had often complained about its tax treatment, it had lived quietly with another problem: the plant's notorious record of labor hostility.

Industrial relations personnel say that more labor grievances were filed in Lackawanna than in all other Bethlehem
plants combined. Caldwell said that when he began labor
relations work at Lackawanna, in 1978, more than forty-five
hundred grievances were in various levels of procedure.
While most were over work-rule nuances, many were inane
and petty complaints. One worker filed a grievance because
the company flew a forty-eight-star flag the day after Hawaii
was admitted to the union.

Members of the dozen or so crafts at Lackawanna jealously
protected their turf by "grieving" at the slightest suspicion of
intrusion. And nowhere were workers quicker to spot openings in antiquated work rules as a way to increase their pay,
already the highest in manufacturing.

"More often than not it was cheaper from a management
standpoint just to say, 'Give the guy four extra hours of pay'
than to fight the issue through grievance procedure," Caldwell said.

Lackawanna might have been saved—at least in the first
wave of shutdowns—if work rules piled on in the bonanza era
had been eased, he felt. "If we could have, we would have
reduced crew sizes," he said. "In almost all the mills, the crew
sizes were much larger than they needed to be. . . . Technological changes would have come sooner and been accepted
better had we had the flexibility."

Sambuchi, of course, violently disagreed. "Give up past
practices? Hell, no," he said. "We tried to give the company
help on its tax problem. But past practices is what it means.
We *fought* for them."

The argument now is academic, of course. Nothing is in
sight to replace the loss of jobs. For those who remain, the tax
burden is punishing. Even with drastic retrenchments, city
taxes went up 29 percent. Even with dwindling school popula-
tions, school taxes have shot up 40 percent. And even with the
stiffest belt-tightening by Ed Rutkowski, Erie County's respected executive, the loss of revenues from Bethlehem Steel

was a major reason Erie County had to ask the legislature in 1984 for new taxing limits to meet mandated programs.

Meanwhile, the young desert the town that their parents and grandparents built. Population has dropped from 28,000 in 1970 to 22,700 today. Neighborhoods disintegrate as once-proud families sell their homes at bargain prices. Speculators buy them up with a minimum down and then milk them as rentals.

Only the renowned Our Lady of Victory Basilica, built by Lackawanna's most famous resident, the late Father Nelson Baker, seems unchanged.

"It is traumatic for a lot of us to see the young go," said Ruth Cullen, parish secretary, who is the widow of a steelworker. "But when you have difficult times, a lot of people turn to the church. Only two bingo games in town have had to close down. And collections at the shrine and the number of candles lit have increased."

With its access to Lake Erie, Lackawanna has better than average resources to offer new employers. Early in 1986, Bethlehem Steel was able to sell 150 acres of the 1,300-acre plant, the section that contains a two hundred-foot wide canal, large enough to handle the biggest ships plying the Great Lakes. The buyers, a newly formed New York company known as Gateway Trade Center, announced no plans except to operate the property as a port facility.

But three years after the shutdown, the city still has no real prescription for recovery. The lessons should be clear enough. Whatever the world economic forces and however shortsighted management decisions may have been, the community of Lackawanna cannot escape its share of blame for the industrial collapse.

Unremitting labor hostility inconsistent with far-seeing union leadership, as well as the local government's taxing insensitivity, created a business climate that today haunts the city fully as much as its empty buildings.

Chapter 18

THE MEANEST
AND THE BEST

THE staff of the United Steelworkers Union in Johnstown operates from a suite of rooms in the Wallace Building on Main Street. The restored structure, which has a Merrill Lynch brokerage office on the ground floor, is in the heart of downtown, a central business district so handsomely refurbished that a visitor does not have the feeling of being in a mill town. But that mood changes at the fourth-floor office of Jerry Groves, USW staff representative.

Groves is a bull of a man with squinty eyes and a cynical smile—the features one might expect of a union organizer who came to Johnstown after battling coal mine owners in West Virginia and shipping tycoons on the waterfronts of New York. At fifty-nine he still has the look of a rugged company foe and apparently cultivates the reputation. A sign on his office wall reads, "Yea, though I walk through the valley of the shadow of death, I shall fear no evil for I am the meanest son-of-a-bitch in the valley."

Over the years, Jerry Groves and his equally militant associates in the USW stamped the union label on Johnstown so thoroughly that the wages, benefits, and security there became a model for the labor movement. Not only did the USW gain ironclad labor control of the Bethlehem complex, the city's largest employer, and the United States Steel works, its second largest employer, but today even bank tellers and dairymen in Johnstown carry USW membership cards.

But Jerry Groves worries about the future. "With the basic steel agreement running out in 1986, from now on everybody is going to go one on one," he complains. "Burns Harbor, Sparrows Point, Steelton, and Johnstown, all Bethlehem plants, are probably going to have separate contracts. Plant will be bucking plant. I don't know where the hell all this is going. The implications will take a decade to work out."

And Jerry Groves knows too well that what is happening at Johnstown could well be fateful for the entire industry. Much has already occurred here to increase the unease of the union. To ailing steel companies looking for new leverage to cut wages and shed restrictive work rules, the Johnstown story is one of the few comforting developments.

When Bethlehem Steel began closing mills and U.S. Steel simply bailed out of Johnstown in 1982, the city fought back —not by militant and largely futile protests against shutdowns but by creative community survival strategies. The cooperation of Johnstown's labor leaders and the sacrifices accepted by the rank and file were cornerstones of that community response. These overtures provided the overriding reason Bethlehem Steel dug in its heels and did not follow U.S. Steel in pulling out of the city.

Perhaps we should not be surprised that labor-management breakthroughs occurred in Johnstown when other distressed cities simply gave up. For a century and a half, furnaces at the Johnstown works, which extends twelve miles down the Conemaugh River, have been making iron and steel despite floods, shifting markets, and changing technology.

Such durability was achieved principally because Johnstown was innovative.

It was here that the first steel rails were produced commercially in the United States, enabling the Pennsylvania Railroad to spread across the state. It was here that the revolutionary Kelly converter, the forerunner of the Bessemer furnace, first converted pig iron into steel. And at a time when scientific development in the steel industry was not ardently pursued, it was here that many new techniques first were developed.

The original Johnstown furnace became the nucleus, in the 1850s, of the Cambria Iron Company. By 1873, Cambria's swift development made it the largest steel plant in America. It continued to expand by acquiring the Gautier Steel Company, which had facilities for making rods, nails, and farm machinery parts. By the turn of the century the facility reorganized as the Cambria Steel Company and continued under that name until Midvale Steel and Ordnance Company gained control of the operation in 1916.

Flush with World War I profits, Bethlehem Steel purchased the Johnstown facility from Midvale in 1923 and rebuilt the plant into a balanced steelmaking unit with six divisions. The integrated mills made steel bars, rails, plates, wire, and an almost endless variety of special shapes that became automobile springs, wheel rims, brake shoes, sled runners, and fence posts. As seen from the air, the plants today line the banks on two sides of a large V created by the intersection of the Conemaugh and the Little Conemaugh rivers.

Nature provided the tremendous quantities of water necessary for steel operations, and bountiful supplies of bituminous coal could be mined from deep veins practically underneath the plant. In fact, the coke works, which converts coal into coke and a variety of byproducts, has a mine shaft right on the property. It was an ideal steel operation. By the start of the 1950s, the Johnstown facility employed about eighteen thousand workers, and they turned out about 2.28 million tons of steel ingots a year.

In the national environmental awakening of the 1970s,

however, the Environmental Protection Agency ordered the steel industry to clean up its emissions, giving it a five-year period to meet primary pollution standards. Johnstown was the oldest facility and therefore required the costliest cleanup, based on its proportion of tonnage capacity.

Rumors spread that Bethlehem would not sink nonproductive capital into an aging plant. In 1973, the company confirmed the fears. It notified management at Johnstown that it would eliminate forty-seven hundred jobs over the next four years as it shut down operations that could not meet the environmental deadline.

A community with lesser tradition might have mistakenly protested by picketing the management gates. But Johnstown set out to save its industry the one way that warms even the coldest corporate heart. It mounted a financial campaign to demonstrate that the community was willing to invest to save itself.

Johnstown's leading citizens—department store owners, publishers, steel executives, and steelworker union leaders—rallied to form Johnstown Area Regional Industries (JARI). Within a year, the group raised $3 million for industrial development. Bethlehem Steel contributed $100,000 outright and matched 50 cents to every dollar raised in the community. Then, heartened by the big upturn in steel demand in 1974 —the industry's last bonanza year—Bethlehem took a new view of the reinvigorated city. It announced it would not only suspend its planned cutbacks in Johnstown, but would also build a basic oxygen furnace shop that would keep the plant in step with all environmental requirements.

However, fears over the future had barely settled down when the torrential flood of 1977 devastated the city and the steel plant.

Once more, Johnstown refused to accept a death sentence. The flood-prone city had survived two such natural disasters before: in 1889 when over two thousand people were killed, and then in 1936. Again a heroic cleanup occurred. Townspeople and swarms of volunteers from outside the city shoveled away mud and debris. Within a few days, life returned to many operations at the Bethlehem Steel plant. Nonetheless, General Manager Thomas Crowley estimated it would take at least $35 million to continue the clean-up.

A delegation from JARI, led by Charles Kunkle, Jr., president of the management firm that operated the Greater Johnstown Water Authority, flew to Bethlehem to visit Kunkle's old friend, Chairman Lewis W. Foy, a Johnstown native, and urged him to allocate funds for the cleanup and renovations.

Foy, whose sister and other relatives still lived in Johnstown, admitted he spent many sleepless nights pondering his decision. With Director William Scranton, the former governor of Pennsylvania, helping to persuade the board, Foy gave Johnstown a second reprieve.

However, the flood did give Bethlehem a face-saving excuse to cancel the basic oxygen project—for which site preparation was already underway. Just prior to the flood, there were well-founded reasons to believe that this process was not suited for Johnstown's product mix and lowered tonnage potential. Two electric furnaces, also designed to meet emission standards, were installed in its place.

Now it was 1982, and new trouble arose. The steel industry was locked in a devastating recession. Companies began closing down older mills all over the country. Bethlehem's severest reductions were in Johnstown and Lackawanna, as previously described, and the remaining operations at both plants were consolidated into one operating unit, the Bar, Rod and Wire Division. But when a decision had to be made as to which plant would supply the steel, the furnaces were phased out, not in Johnstown, but in Lackawanna.

Obviously, Johnstown had always been something more than another plant for Bethlehem Steel. It was hardly an accident, therefore, that the company concentrated on Johnstown as the place to establish a new era of labor relations. Bethlehem knew that profitability could not return without shedding restrictive work rules, and without a greater scaledown of wages and benefits beyond the those negotiated with Joe Odorcich in early 1983. The only course open now was to seek plant-by-plant concessions.

The cultivation started with a program to break down the years of union-company hostility in the mills. Donald Trautlein formed Labor-Management Participation Teams (LMPTs) shortly after he became chairman of Bethlehem Steel in 1980. The objective was to invite workers on the floor to share ideas on how to improve products and efficiency. The LMPTs had uneven acceptance, but at Johnstown friendly sit-and-discuss meetings evolved into programs where hourly workers became so interested in improving product and performance that they willingly went to customer plants to hear complaints and discuss needs directly with the buyers.

Early in 1983, Bethlehem Steel notified the union that Johnstown had to have a separate contract to survive. Surprisingly, the International Steelworkers headquarters in Johnstown agreed. With only three thousand men working and another three thousand on layoff, Jerry Groves conceded there was little choice. "We got the authorization to renegotiate a local contract here," he said.

Memories of the anguish over that renegotiation were still fresh in December 1985, when I dropped into the offices of USW Franklin Local 2635. Franklin represents the primary mills, the electric furnaces, and the remainder of the rolling mills—the bulk of the labor force at the Johnstown plant.

"They had what they called the 'Brown Book,'" Ron Davies, the financial secretary recalled. "Someone did a study that showed jobs that could be eliminated, and the company said that had to happen for the plant to stay alive. What they did was combine jobs. For example, where we had a crew with a loader and three chainmen, they came back and said, 'We don't need the third chainman. The loader can come by and pick up the slack.' So they eliminate one man on each crew there.

"Then they go to the grinder's complex where there are four cranemen on duty. They say we don't need four cranes running at one time. First, they cut it down to three cranes and then they cut it down to two. At the Number Three yard, they eliminated about four chainmen and picked up the slack by making the inspectors and loaders and whoever else was in the yard take turns helping chain. They just doubled up jobs."

In 1959, when the industry last tried to remove archaic work rules from the steelworkers' contract, the union successively defied the challenge by calling a strike that lasted 116 days. Now in 1983, Bethlehem changed the work rules in every plant in Johnstown and not a day's work stoppage resulted.

True, Franklin Local 2635, the first to vote on the package, rejected it on the first ballot. Bethlehem threatened to end steelmaking in Johnstown if the package was turned down a second time. Sixteen days later, Franklin voted to accept the concessions by a margin of three to one. The remaining four locals soon approved similar "Save the Mills" agreements.

"This should prove to the people of Johnstown that we are not a greedy bunch," Charles Molnar, then president of Local 2635, said in an interview with the *Tribune-Democrat*, Johnstown's daily newspaper. "We may be a bit hardheaded but steelworkers also have the welfare of the city at heart." Molnar added that he did not believe that Bethlehem was bluffing in its threat to close the plant.

Early in 1985, eighteen months later, the union locals in Johnstown were tested anew. By now, Bethlehem Steel was enduring its fourth straight year of losses. Despite cost reductions and labor-saving practices, Johnstown still was among the unprofitable operations. Once more ultimatums came from the home office: Bethlehem would put no more money into Johnstown unless it showed a profit by the end of the year.

That meant closing the gap between the $24-an-hour labor costs at the Bar, Rod and Wire Division and the $14-an-hour average paid by the minimills, many of which not only have no unions but operate with cost-saving continuous casters. However, instead of simply asking for outright wage concessions, Bethlehem offered a profit-sharing and stock option plan to make up for compensation cuts.

To Jack Sabo, the slender treasurer of Franklin Local 2635, Johnstown workers were being asked for sacrifices that even the striking workers of failing Wheeling-Pittsburgh Steel Company had rejected after their company filed under Chapter 11 of the federal bankruptcy laws. "They told us they needed $2.52 cents an hour more," Sabo said. "They threatened to shut us down if they couldn't get it."

Nonetheless, on March 23, 1985, the lead story in the *Tribune-Democrat* reported that all six locals in the Bar, Rod and Wire Division, including the five in Johnstown, had approved by a two to one majority a cost-saving agreement "that probably saved the Johnstown operation."

Sabo insisted the cuts came closer to $4.50 an hour than the $2.52 estimated by the company. (The Wheeling-Pittsburgh concession, coming only after a three-month strike in 1985, was estimated at $3.40.) Some Johnstown employees in incentive jobs, he said, gave up $10,000 a year to keep working. Sabo produced a copy of the contract for my inspection. While it was impossible to pin down a specific dollar amount on the concessions, I could see the contract was probably the most revolutionary ever reached between a plant and a major steel company.

Under a heading "Joint Effort Toward Success," the agreement contained a preamble for the need for sacrifices "from each of us" and contained the following specifics:

• Direct pay cuts. All hourly rates were reduced by 82 cents per hour and the wage increase of 45 cents an hour due February 1, 1986, under the basic steel agreement, was cancelled. In exchange, preference stock equal to the cost of the value of this reduction was to be paid pursuant to an employee investment program. [At the annual stockholders meeting soon after, Bethlehem Steel was authorized to issue up to 20 million shares of a new class of preference stock for this purpose. The stock was to be held in a trust to be distributed to an employee at the separation of employment or to his heirs after death. Each employee was to receive a monthly report on the amount of his or her investment.]

• Elimination of incentive pay. That meant discontinuing the extra wages provided under the basic steel agreement when crews exceed the normal output predetermined by time studies of their operation. A profit-sharing plan was established to replace up to the first $1 per hour of incentive earnings. Incentive earnings greater than $1 an hour were to be replaced with preference stock.

• Reduced vacations. Employees with three or more weeks of vacation eligibility lost two weeks. One week was eliminated for employees with two weeks of eligibility. In each case, the cuts were effective for 1986 and 1987.

• Reduced holidays. The ten holidays were cut to seven, eliminating Washington's Birthday, Good Friday, and the day after Thanksgiving. In exchange, preference stock equal to the value of this concession was issued to the employee.

• Reduced health care. Vision care insurance and the dental plan were eliminated. A mandatory second surgical opinion was established for thirteen classes of elective surgical procedures.

• Lower shift premiums. The premiums of 30 cents and 45 cents per hour [paid to those who worked middle and night shifts respectively] were reduced 10 cents and 25 cents. The holiday premium of two and one-half times an hour was cut to double time, and the Sunday premium was eliminated. In exchange, preference stock again was to be paid to qualifying employees.

For its part in the joint effort toward success, Bethlehem Steel made two principal commitments. One was a binding promise to spread the sacrifices by reducing salaried employee compensation by $845,000 per year, or an average cut of $1,706 per year for each white-collar worker. The other was a not-so-binding promise to recommend the installation of a continuous caster at Johnstown, "once the division has shown that it can maintain adequate profitability, if there is economic and technological justification for a caster, and if satisfactory financing is available."

The equal-sacrifice commitment lent a strong good-faith element to the agreement. However, union workers in their hearts realized that the promise of a continuous caster was not really in the cards. Bethlehem had started to build a four-strand billet caster in Johnstown during the early 1970s, when it had profits to invest, but then cancelled the project with the caster 90 percent completed. The limited space around the Johnstown plant was physically ill-suited for an investment that would devour more than $100 million; there is every reason to believe its caster will never be operational.

Workers in Johnstown made lopsided sacrifices to save their plant. Was the price worth it? The hard core in the union view the concessions as the emasculation of the union card. These workers argue that the company bought "yes" votes by offering $400-a-month pensions and revising age and service qualifications to make it easier to retire. "The older workers voted for it just to get out, and a lot of young people on layoff voted for it just to get back to work," says Ron Davies, financial secretary of Franklin Local 2635.

Davies, along with other critics, charges that Bethlehem Steel dragged its feet on the equal-sacrifice commitment to reduce white collar salaries by $845,000 a year. By year end in 1985, several locals ordered members to boycott the labor-management participation sessions until the company proved good faith.

Meanwhile, every union local president who endorsed the concessions paid the price. Charles Molnar and his counterparts were voted out of office in the union elections that occurred a month later. The only local president to survive was Raymond Jastrzab of Lower Cambria, and he had opposed the concessions. His was a special case because the new contract wiped out job security agreements that had been separately negotiated for Lower Cambria.

The new union officers find little joy in their ouster of the incumbents. They know that they, too, will have to make difficult choices as unprofitability continues.

"A couple of years ago the biggest fear in this town was the rain," Sabo said. "Every time it rained, we worried whether the South Fork Dam would break. Now the big worry is when someone says, 'I hear Trautlein is coming to town.' It's the same damn thing. The dam is going to break or Trautlein is going to make more cuts. The town is running scared one way or the other."

However, the union's pain is not reflected in the city of Johnstown. I heard only expressions of community pride for a union that had the courage to face realities. The important thing to the townspeople was that the Johnstown plant, at least what's left of it, again was saved. Further, the union vote helped spread the message that Johnstown has a labor climate conducive to healthy industry.

Larger economic factors are going to determine whether steelmaking in Johnstown survives permanently. But the city did its share, and so did the union. Bethlehem Steel has been kept alive there on the joint sacrifices of its concerned people.

Chapter 19

WHEN THE WORKERS BUY THE COMPANY

THE steel town of Weirton, West Virginia, is an easy forty-five-minute drive from Pittsburgh, long the capital of steel-making in the United States. In terms of sophistication, the gap is considerably wider. Culture-minded and diverse, Pittsburgh enjoys Three River Arts Festivals and a world-class civic symphony at Heinz Hall. Dominated by a single smoke-stack industry, Weirton is a workingman's community where mourning families still hang funeral wreaths on the front door and the American Legion is a big civic force. Yet Weirton overshadows Pittsburgh in one important way.

While the steel mills along the rivers forming Pittsburgh's triangle have been slumping or closing since 1983, Weirton Steel has been thriving. And while nervous unions have been girding for plant-by-plant showdowns with steel companies seeking concessions, Weirton has put labor showdowns be-hind it and is concentrating on turning out new products that are making a statement in the marketplace.

There is one more significant distinction. Weirton is employee-owned, the largest steel plant in the country to be acquired in an employee buyout. It was purchased from National Steel Corporation in 1983 for $386 million. The raising of that kind of money by Weirton's seven thousand employees defies belief—until you discover that the United States government pitched in.

Weirton's purchase was made possible by an Employee Stock Ownership Plan (ESOP), which was born of legislation passed by Congress in the early 1970s and bolstered by additional laws granting further tax incentives to participating companies. In short, ESOPs actually allow employees to buy their company without putting up cash. A trust fund is created that lends money to the operating company. The company deposits its common stock with the trust as collateral for the loan. The company pays back its loan to the trust out of operating income with payments that are tax deductible. And as the stock is paid off, it is allocated to participating employees according to their relative compensation.

A principal architect of the Weirton Steel employee takeover in 1983 was a silver-haired, bespectacled executive named Jack Redline, then in his early sixties. Jack was a classmate of mine in the late 1930s at Nazareth High School, which is ten rural miles away from Bethlehem. In those years, most high school graduates in that limestone and farming region went directly to jobs in a cement mill or on the farm. The really lucky ones were hired at "the Steel."

Jack, whose father was a janitor at Nazareth Cement, was doubly lucky. First he survived fifty-one European bombing missions on a B-17 in World War II, during which he attained the rank of captain. Then he entered Lehigh University to study engineering, aided by a part-time job at Bethlehem Steel, which was the equivalent of a scholarship.

As a 235-pound tackle on Lehigh's football team, Redline was a tough and heady player. Few pro scouts ever visit the Lehigh stadium, but top-level Bethlehem Steel executives make the games a Saturday afternoon ritual whenever the team is playing at home. They quickly noticed Redline. As soon as he graduated in 1948, they recruited him for the loop course, the management training program.

But Redline soon found the pace at staid Bethlehem Steel too slow. Opportunities for engineers were plentiful in the post–World War II years, so he switched companies in 1959, landing at National Steel, the fourth largest producer, as an assistant superintendent of its new finishing plant in Indiana. He was promoted swiftly at National and participated in the design and construction of the industry's earliest continuous casters, first at National's Weirton Steel subsidiary and later at National's Great Lakes plant near Detroit.

Redline was sent back to Weirton in 1977 to tackle the plant's mounting operational problems, which had "chewed up" three previous presidents in fast succession. He put the plant into the black in his first full year. It was still profitable, but evidently not profitable enough, when he received a confidential call from the home office in January of 1982. He was told that Weirton either would be closed or become an employee-owned facility.

Two months later, Jack Redline broke the news to the employees.

In the minds of workers, the word "buyout" automatically stirs fears of pay cuts and pension erosion. However, one of the most enthusiastic supporters of the buyout idea was Redline. That blunted the instant critics because he was much respected in Weirton, mixing with the steelworkers at church suppers, Little League games, and on the tees of the Elks golf course.

"Jack Redline was one of the family," one worker said. "He not only remembered my first name, but he knew my wife when he spotted her in town and always asked about the kids, whose names he also remembered."

His management style was just as down-to-earth. He personally met with all the shop stewards once a month to discuss grievances and never passed up an opportunity to praise an employee for good performance. When anyone saved a piece of equipment or averted an accident in the shop, Redline presented the employee with a Finger-in-the-Dike Award and took the worker and guests to dinner.

As an insider, Redline knew that National Steel wanted to lessen its dependence on steelmaking. An in-depth survey of the steel industry in 1980 showed that while Weirton was profitable, it was clearly vulnerable to the negative forces descending on the industry. That persuaded National to start phasing out its oldest plant.

Redline was not convinced of the validity of the decision. He was certain that Weirton Steel was in better shape to weather hard times than the larger integrated mills. It had a jump on the industry in cost-saving technology, having installed a continuous caster in 1968 when most major firms still suspected the process. It had become one of the biggest tin producers in the nation, gaining a commanding 20 percent market share. Furthermore, it had a reputation for quality.

Most importantly, Weirton had a labor force where generations of families worked side by side, with no international union exacerbating labor relations. The Independent Steelworkers Union represented the plant and office employees. All disputes were settled in-family.

The steel plant also was located in a strongly supportive community. Ernest T. Weir started the operation in 1909 in what was then a remote section of the Upper Ohio Valley. The mill has since become the largest employer in West Virginia and the community of Weirton has grown to twenty-six thousand people. The livelihoods of nearly all the residents are affected either directly or indirectly by the plant. If there was a chance of saving Weirton Steel through the strange-sounding ESOP plan, the banks, businessmen, and townspeople could be expected to go all out to help the workers.

Management and labor formed a joint study committee within three days of National's announcement. Redline took his place on the committee, side by side with Independent Steelworkers Union president Richard "Red" Arango, who was named co-chairman. However, a credible study required money, and it was clear that the initial flush of contributions from company executives and the union strike fund would not be nearly enough to cover the fees necessary to hire the right consultants.

The Joint Study Committee was incorporated as a not-for-profit corporation and launched a general fund-raising campaign. Redline talked proudly about the response during a lengthy interview over lunch in February of 1985. "Money came in from vendors, businessmen, and civic leaders, and the employees themselves put up $60 apiece to get this concept started," he said.

Under banners of "We Can Do It," the community conducted sock hops, bake sales, and a twelve-hour telethon in cash-raising efforts that captured attention and sympathy. *Fortune* magazine recognized the effort, sending a reportorial team into town during the spring of 1983 to do an article entitled, "A Steel Town's Bid to Save Itself."

The money was quickly put to use. Some $500,000 went toward hiring the McKinsey Company consulting firm. Five months later, McKinsey delivered its findings: Weirton Steel products had a solid, if reduced, future in the marketplace. While the plant did ship upward of 2.4 million tons of steel in 1981–1982, it could expect shipments of only about 1.7 million tons through 1984 and only slight growth afterward. It was a disappointing prognosis, but not entirely discouraging.

Then came the projection that tested Weirton's will: an estimated $1 billion would be needed to modernize the plant if it was to remain competitive, and only a 32 percent cut in wages and benefits could enable the reorganized company to amass such cash flow.

Weirton employees were the highest paid in the steel industry, earning about $3 an hour more than steelworkers paid under the coordinated agreement binding the major steel producers. They made between $40,000 and $45,000 a year in wages and benefits, largely because of the premium Na-

tional paid to keep out organizing efforts by the United Steelworkers.

However, a 32 percent cut was hard to accept. That translated into about an $8-an-hour giveback, unheard of even in
failing companies. The drive to save Weirton noticeably
weakened. Many workers now echoed the original militants:
"We can't afford to take any reductions in what we worked so
hard to get." Indeed, a number of rebelling workers had
already filed lawsuits to enjoin the proposed sale to employees, charging that it would deprive them of pensions and
severance rights.

Redline spent days and nights shoring up the sagging
campaign. The alternative to an employee buyout was
harsher, he argued, and he spread that message to every civic
club and church group that would listen to him. "This is the
only way our jobs are going to be saved," he insisted. "Don't
let emotions set a trap for good judgment."

Workers began to reserve judgment, waiting to see what
National was going to offer in the buyout. To exact the best
terms from the parent company, the committee again reached
deep into its publicly raised funds. It retained Willkie Farr and
Gallagher, a New York law firm, and Lazard Freres Company,
the investment banking house, to conduct the negotiations.
Redline said this stratagem turned the tide.

"We got National Steel to absorb 12 percent [of the 32
percent costs to be made up by employee givebacks] by agreeing to pick up certain pensions and retiree life insurance and
health care benefits," he said. "That meant workers now had
to make up only 20 percent. Instead of an $8-an-hour cut, it
was now down to about $5 an hour. That was still hard to
accept, especially for older workers who believed they would
do better by just closing the company and taking their pensions." However, Redline kept arguing, even with a $5-an-
hour cut, Weirton workers would still be making at least $5
an hour more than any other jobs in the area could possibly
pay them.

Redline now began to feel that the deal could succeed. He

knew that the cost-reduction figure could not be shaved. His own calculation in 1981–1982 showed that Weirton Steel wage costs were $13 an hour more than the Japanese, the principal foreign competitor, while the manhours a ton were about even. Considering that Japanese steelmakers had to spend about $40 a ton to ship their product to American markets, slicing wage costs down by a total of $8 an hour per man would be, by his calculation, just enough to make Weirton competitive.

"The workers understood," Redline said. "We negotiated a six-year contract with no raises for six years." The proposed give-backs for hourly workers came to a 19.57 percent cut in pay and fewer days off, while salaried employees faced a cut of 20.9 percent in pay and benefits. In return, said Redline, "there was an equity position and profit sharing. I venture to say that in three years from now they will be as well off as they were before."

On March 12, 1983, a tentative agreement was reached on the specific terms for the compensation to National Steel. National agreed to turn over all assets to Weirton employees for $386.1 million with a payment of $74.7 million in cash up front. Employees were to assume all short-range and long-term debts, which amounted to $192.3 million. National was to issue two promissory notes to Weirton, one for $47.2 million, due in 1993, and a second for $72 million, due in 1998. A final contractual statement provided that if Weirton should "fail substantially" during the next five years, National would assume fiscal responsibility.

The agreement was greeted in Weirton with "relief bordering on glee," *Fortune* magazine reported. National Steel, too, had reason to rejoice. No one questioned too strongly, if at all, how failing "substantially"—the condition that would force National to come back—was to be defined. Meanwhile, National received a decent price for an unwanted mill and saved itself $400 million in pension payouts.

The outcome was a foregone conclusion when the total package was put to a vote by Weirton's eight thousand eligible steelworkers—including the one thousand on layoff—in September. Three separate issues had to be approved—the six-year labor agreement with wage cut concessions, a new pension plan, and the stock ownership formula. All three segments were overwhelmingly accepted.

"It's a big day for Weirton," Bill Bowen, a millwright for twenty-eight years, told the press in a typical post-election reaction. "After today we'll be in business and we'll have to make a buck."

For Jack Redline the victory was tempered by sadness; he was denied the opportunity to complete what he had started. Some months before the decisive vote, an eight-member board was appointed to run the employee-owned company upon completion of the acquisition. The unions filled three seats, and five independent directors, all nationally prominent businessmen and lawyers, were approved on the recommendations of the Joint Study Committee's investment banker, Lazard Freres. (Ironically, one of these seats went to Richard Schubert, the former president and vice chairman of Bethlehem Steel who left Bethlehem in the Trautlein executive exodus and then became president of the American Red Cross.)

The first major act of the new board was to choose a president for the new Weirton Steel. The management consulting firm of Heidrick Struggles, Incorporated, conducted a nationwide recruiting search. Redline, now sixty-two, was one of four finalists and went to New York for a three-hour interview by the board but didn't get the job. The appointment went to Robert L. Loughhead, an accountant who was president of Copperweld Steel Company—and who was nine years younger.

Redline conceded his disappointment in not becoming the new company's first president but said he had no regrets about his buy-back efforts. And apparently the respect he won in Weirton is now statewide. Early in 1985, West Virginia Govenor Arch A. Moore, Jr., tapped Redline to become a member of his cabinet, with the title of Director of State Development.

Is the Weirton ESOP a case study in survival for other steel plants in trouble?

"What Weirton proved," Redline said, "is that employees can save their steel mill if the right ingredients for survival are there. You have to have a willing parent company. And the plant has to be viable, with a proven ability to compete, particularly in quality. And you need a dedicated work force willing to do what it has to."

Since Weirton, the popularity of buy-backs has grown as a way of saving failing plants or involving workers in a share of the profits. The *New York Times* reported that the number of stock ownership and bonus plans had climbed by the end of 1984 to more than 5,700 covering 9.6 million workers—in comparison to 843 plans covering 520,000 workers in 1976. Not in all cases do workers control their companies, of course. Sometimes ESOPs are used to give employees only partial ownership, and in recent years giving workers a major block of stock under the plan has become part of a strategy of avoiding hostile takeovers.

The growth of ESOPs has drawn support—and opposition—from all points of the political compass. The concept comes under attack from the free enterprise purists who argue that the plans make government a partner in bailing out weak companies, those that can't survive without the tax benefits and wage concessions that become part of the rescue.

J. Bruce Johnston, executive vice president of U.S. Steel, is among these critics. He is against ESOPs in the industry because he feels the tax breaks given to the employee-owned companies penalize steel's healthier companies, which must compete without equal tax advantages.

Since the basic ESOP authorizing-laws in 1973, however, Congress has carried the tax breaks several steps farther, tacking on at least fifteen other major pieces of legislation encouraging their use. For example, in 1984 it exempted from taxable income half of the interest banks earn on loans to the plans, thereby further inciting the critics.

Redline said that during the campaign to save Weirton

Steel he became well aware of hostility over the concept of employee ownership. "I got letters from all over accusing us of fostering socialism," he said. "We classified it as fostering survival. Besides, the idea is to establish *capitalists*. We added seven thousand capitalists on the rolls at Weirton."

Meanwhile, the seven thousand new steel-plant owners at Weirton and the townspeople there couldn't be more delighted. A visitor can't escape the town's special spirit. On the way to the plant, a bank's neon sign, which normally proclaims the prevailing interest rate, was flashing the message, "Let's Buy Steel."

At the plant, President Loughhead held a press tour early in December 1985 to announce that Weirton Steel had become the first producer in the United States to produce a new galvanized sheet that offers superior resistance to corrosion. As I watched these wide sheets streaming through a mill the length of a football field, John MacDonald, a thirty-two-year veteran steelmaker who is general manager of the operation, remarked that business at Weirton was the best since 1974.

The upbeat attitude in the Weirton mill was in sharp contrast to the demoralized attitude so prevalent at most Bethlehem Steel plants and union offices. Beaming workers told me how the idea to produce the new galvanized product was conceived in August and was on the production line by December, a feat that would be unheard of in a conventionally structured plant with its layers of corporate bureaucracy.

"How long would it have taken if you still had to go through National?" I asked.

"The plans would still be sitting somewhere in Pittsburgh," MacDonald said, referring to National Steel's home offices.

Since becoming an employee-owned company, Weirton has returned a profit every quarter, earning $60.6 million in 1984 when nearly every integrated steel mill was reporting losses. "Workers probably miss the wages they gave back," Loughhead said during the press tour. "But the feeling is good . . . we expect a profitable fourth quarter and another profitable year."

Weirton casts another ray of hope for an embattled industry. The steelworkers there have shown one way that an old but still viable steel plant can survive. For the larger companies, the formula for survival is more elusive, but there are, nonetheless, lessons in what Weirton proved.

Chapter 20

PINNING THE BLAME

A common perception is that big steel is in trouble because it is under siege from world forces it can no longer control. That is only partially true. I am convinced that the biggest cause for the industry's distress is the internal strife that saps its strength from within. Accordingly, the greatest hope for its recovery rests not on what is happening on the outside but on whether steel management and labor can recognize—and recognize soon—that they have to stop killing each other.

Perhaps no industry has had such a sustained history of hostile labor relations. For more than forty-five years, ever since the United Steelworkers Union of America organized the mills, the companies and the union have been battling in public and private, and often as though each confrontation was a fight to the finish. Even now, as major steel firms file for protection from creditors and teeter on the brink of bankruptcy, the two sides are going at it with the same adversarial fervor.

No one represents the antagonists in this deep-rooted conflict better than two men with offices within a few blocks of each other in Pittsburgh's Golden Triangle. On the sixty-first floor of the U.S. Steel Building at 600 Grant Street sits J. Bruce Johnston, fifty-two, the urbane executive vice president of the nation's largest steel producer. He has been the chief contract negotiator for the coordinated steel companies for more than a decade. Holding court on the twelfth floor of United Steelworkers Union Building at Five Gateway Center is Lynn R. Williams, sixty, the comparatively new leader of the steel industry's dominant union, whom *Business Week* once described as "one of the fastest rising stars in the labor movement."

Johnston, the son of a steelworker, grew up in Donora, Pennsylvania, a steel town along the Monongahela River in western Pennsylvania. While the cut of his suits and his sophisticated wit reflect the influence of a Harvard Law School education, he never ceases to remind interviewers of his Donora background, proudly claiming that he spent more time working in a steel mill than union boss Williams.

"On a personal basis, I like Lynn," Johnston told me in December of 1985, as he began assessing the people and the forces in the industry's decline. "He has middle-class poise. He has a masters degree in sociology. At contract time, he genuinely wants to save every union member. The problem is, he has to choose from flawed options. 'Whatever the boys want, I'm behind them.' That's Williams. I contend that's a strange piece of geography for a leader. It's like a general saying, 'I've got to find out where my army is so I can catch up to them and lead them.'"

Williams, a gentle man who, some say, doesn't have an obscenity in his vocabulary, speaks in the abstract. The son of a Protestant lay preacher, he is a native of Canada where he had a career as a union organizer until winning a rung on the international ladder with the Lloyd McBride ticket in 1977. He is well aware of Johnston's disdain for his leadership style.

"Bruce is a one-theme critic," Williams says. "He knows full well that USW presidents don't negotiate contracts. We have a staff of lawyers, accountants, and researchers who have a continuity that dates back farther than when Johnston started."

With that civilized sparring out of the way, both men talk seriously and often bitterly of the deeply rooted differences that have kept industry labor relations in constant turmoil. Each draws a diametrically different picture, of course, in the crucial areas where blame must be assigned.

Johnston's position is that neither the union nor much of the American public understands the basis of the industry's distress. He sees the problems as "deep-seated, structural, and political" in their origin and stresses that it is important to view them in a perspective that starts with why Andrew Carnegie, the father of U.S. Steel, left the beautiful town of Dunfermline, Scotland, to come to the obscure Monongahela Valley in 1848.

"Carnegie's father was a successful weaver who was wiped out overnight by an invention that melded steam power to the flying shuttle," Johnston says. "That was good for the rest of the world but it was hard on the Carnegie family. So that drove them to America."

The story of how Andrew Carnegie rose from a message runner in Pittsburgh to the founder of U.S. Steel is an often-told saga. However, Johnston points out that Carnegie soon did to many tradesmen what the steam-driven shuttle did to his father, and sees continuing parallels in today's world.

"Remember, Carnegie grew up in a cottage industry," Johnston says. "And what he found here [in America] was that steelmaking also was a cottage industry. One guy owned a coal mine, another a limestone quarry. Somebody else had wagons. Others puddled iron. A few guys with thimble-sized pots were converting iron into steel. Carnegie saw a way to make it vastly more efficient by consolidating the operations.

He got the license for a Bessemer converter and he built the world's first integrated steel mill. That was good for Americans but overnight it destroyed the European steel industry.

"Now we come down to the new structural changes, the ones undermining the health of our industry today. When Carnegie and, after him, Charlie Schwab among the other pioneers, built the present steel industry, there were several critical factors that enabled them to be competitive."

Johnston maintains the single most important advantage was not inexpensive labor—he lists that as second—but the cost of capital. "That's where we're hurting the most today," he adds. "We're having a very difficult time competing against cheap capital worldwide. We went through years where it took twelve years to recover a capital investment in steel mills, rolling mills, blast furnaces, and so on. If you put $100 million into a rolling mill in 1960 and you run the hell out of it for twelve years, look what happens when you go to replace it. You've been allowed to recover $100 million but by now it costs $300 million to replace that mill. You can't do it. Meanwhile, capital recovery time in Europe is five years, in Canada it's two years, and the United Kingdom one year. And in the Pacific basin and Third World countries, capital support for the steel mills has been unlimited.

"The transcendent reality is that we have overbuilt the steel industry worldwide. We have 300 million tons more annual capacity every year than there is annual demand. As long as you have 600 million tons of demand chasing 900 million tons of capacity, you're never going to get the price for your product that will allow you to survive."

Johnston lists more major structural changes that have staggered American steelmaking. "Our labor costs became the highest in the world; the pure iron ore from the Mesabi range ran out, thereby eliminating an important natural resource advantage; and OPEC did it to us on energy costs. Our energy bill is eleven times higher than General Motors'. We are the largest energy consumer in the United States. Lastly, we have lost the literacy advantage. The average Japanese high school grad knows twice as much math, twice as much science, and has twice as many engineering skills as the average high school grad here. Their craftsmen have leapfrogged us."

Johnston contends that not only has the United Steelworkers Union failed to concede the impact of these structural changes in any meaningful contract concessions, but the union has such a structural problem of its own that its leaders cannot address them fearlessly if they wish to stay in office.

"We get the union reps in here, tell them our problem, and they say, 'Yep, too bad.' But nobody wants to be the guy who stands up and says, 'I think we're going to have to moderate our packages.' Because he won't get elected. Because there is always a guy who will stand up and say, 'Hey, don't vote for that bastard. We don't need concessions, this company's still got money. We ought to get more.' " Johnston was not surprised to learn that all three local presidents who supported the concessions at Bethlehem Steel's Johnstown plant were promptly voted out of office at the next election.

To underscore his point about the importance of self-preservation in union decision making, Johnston whips out a fifty-eight-page report listing the payroll of the United Steelworkers, which it files with the Department of Labor. Then he reads off name after name of union employees drawing compensation ranging from $28,000 for routine office workers to $108,000 for people who are not even international officers.

"You can do very well if you're a local president. Take Phil Cyprian out at Gary," he continues. "Phil Cyprian was making $94,000 in this 1983 list, not counting the generous pension [contribution] we paid him, or the insurance and health benefits on top of that. Now if he loses the election, he's back to his scarfing job in the mill. There'll be no local mayor seeking him out, no congressman asking advice, no *Wall Street Journal* reporter calling for quotes. Hell, he wants to hang on, and Lynn wants to hang on. Well, for many a local union guy, the way to hang on, if you're challenged, is to damn and demagogue the company.

"Lynn Williams doesn't have the guts politically to say to his people, 'Hey, that train went by. This plant has worked out its useful life. There is no replacement capital for it.' [The union] expects us to cannibalize the rest of the corporation to keep a plant running while it yields nothing.

"Lynn Williams is president of a no-fault union. They feel they don't have to do much about anything except shout through bullhorns at rallies and bitch about Roderick [U.S. Steel Chairman David Roderick], President Reagan, the trade enforcement agencies, and everyone else while claiming they have done nothing wrong. Nonsense. They were very good at helping to divide the pie, but they didn't create the pie. It wasn't their capital, their technology, or their risk."

U.S. Steel clearly does not like the odds that those attitudes will change. It has accelerated a major move away from steel-making. In 1982, it bought Marathon Oil for close to $6 billion and in 1986 it sought to acquire Texas Oil and Gas Corporation for about $3.6 billion. Robert R. Reich of Harvard's John F. Kennedy School of Government is among those who have written that U.S. Steel will someday change its name, "maybe to U.S. Energy." (The change was to U.S. X.)

I walked down the hill on that chilly December day to Five Gateway Center and posed Johnston's scathing indictments to Lynn Williams. Having interviewed or met every steel-worker union president since Phil Murray, I found it hard at first to believe that this man—humble, philosophical, bespec-tacled—was boss of that tough breed of worker who labors in the nation's mills. However, in his own quiet way, Williams spoke with great force for the union position, indicting John-ston and other industry leaders for their role in prolonging the hostility.

If steelworker locals elect officers with hard-nosed atti-tudes toward the company, Williams contended, it is because of the management they have to deal with. "I think the com-pany essentially determines the tone of those relationships, and the workers elect the kind of officers who they perceive will be tough enough to deal with [the situation]."

Williams insisted that it was only when steel companies approached the brink of insolvency that management attitudes changed significantly. "For a long time, they ruled with total arrogance in the plants," he said. "They said to workers, 'Look, we're not interested in your ideas, we're not interested in your suggestions, we want you just to punch the time clock and do what your boss says. He's always right, and he knows everything.'

"The steel companies shut American workers, their ideas, and their creativity out of the system. Now labor-management participation is supposed to overcome that terrible error of so many years."

Williams claimed that the union spends more time worrying about the viability of the steel industry than collective bargaining, at least in the traditional sense. "We are much more interested these days in having workers have more control over what happens in the industry . . . for example, to fight for plant-shutdown legislation, to have more shop-floor democracy, and to persuade companies to put union members on the boards of directors."

What of the charge that the union is not assuming its proper burden in helping the industry survive?

"Essentially, we have reaffirmed that the union is not interested in going backward," he said. "We're not interested in reducing our standard of living. We don't think that makes a contribution either to the companies or the general public. There seem to be too many people out there who are neglecting the idea that a prosperous society needs a good base of consumers to keep that prosperity going. Most economists will agree that what prosperity has been created in the Reagan years has been consumption driven. We want to maintain decent wages and standards."

Even if a company goes broke paying for them?

"We don't have our head in the sand on this issue. When dire economic circumstances exist, we will attempt to deal with them. We have certain standards to apply. One, such a company has to make its information totally available to qua-

lified experts whom we hire. Two, [there has] to be an appropriate quid pro quo. We look at stock as one appropriate thing
the company can give in return."

Do you expect to see Bruce Johnston coming at you, I
asked, demanding that U.S. Steel get the same $4 or $5 an
hour wage concession you gave to its competitor, Wheeling-
Pitt, to save it from bankruptcy?

"We don't see a pattern being set for an industry on the
basis of a bankrupt participant . . . there are no level playing
fields in this industry."

What are the union's criteria for reversing the crisis in the
industry?

"The crisis is whether we are going to maintain an industrial base in this society or not. Whether we are going to use
the talents of American workers, nourish them, and remain a
productive society that makes goods, or whether we are to
become simply a society that services other people. I think it
would be a terrible mistake to let [the latter] happen. Instead
of being the leader in the world we would become hostage to
many other countries. Are we to depend on the Japanese, the
Koreans, the Brazilians, the Europeans to defend our country? We need to make a deliberate decision that we are going
to preserve our basic industry."

Two months later, Bethlehem Steel, reporting its fourth
straight year of losses, called upon the United Steelworkers to
forego a 45-cents-an hour raise due on February 1, 1986,
under terms of the "concessionary contract" negotiated in
1983. The union refused. Soon afterward, U.S. Steel dis-
tanced itself even farther from steelmaking—and Andrew
Carnegie's commitment—when its shareholders formally approved the $3.6 billion deal to acquire Texas Oil and Gas.

Chapter 21

CAN IT BE SAVED?

FOR the people of Bethlehem, it is no longer possible to ignore the fact that they may lose their steel plant. The once-steady roar from Bethlehem Steel is reduced to a murmur. At least half of the five-mile-long steelmaking complex along the Lehigh River resembles a wasteland.

On many afternoons, grim-faced people pause on the New Street Bridge and look down the river bank to see what is happening to Bethlehem Steel. Old-timers shake their heads sadly at the sight. Demolition crews have flattened the merchant mills, now leaving only piles of rubble where, since the early 1900s, thousands of workers once heated, chipped, and rolled strips of steel into shapes. At the far end of the plant, a tool shop, modernized only twenty years ago, looks simply abandoned. Expensive equipment is rusting, and pigeon droppings cover idled rolling tables where streams of steel billets used to flow.

The scene is one of giant, crane-borne buckets rusting

among disconnected motors, in a facility where as late as 1982 teams of hard-hatted men forged 250-ton stone-crushers and big turbine castings for the likes of General Electric and Westinghouse. A half-dozen silent diesel locomotives sit frozen on their tracks, stark symbols of an industry waiting for a wake-up signal.

While the city of Bethlehem did have the vision to begin industrial diversification twenty-five years ago, no property owner there has escaped the pain of steel's deterioration. Taxes have gone up sharply to make up for the $14 million cut in Bethlehem Steel's tax assessment. Retail sales are down and even old reliable institutions are hurting. In 1986, the *Globe-Times* had to suspend its Sunday newspaper for lack of advertising. Jim Davis, the popular executive director of the Bethlehem Area Chamber of Commerce, left his job because of forced budget cuts. The city's United Way agency eliminated jobs and human services as Bethlehem Steel's support shrank from $1.5 million annually to $625,000. A blue daze characterizes the mood of this town. By now, the thousands of dismissed or involuntarily retired steel employees have discovered that it is impossible to find jobs that pay as well as the ones at steel.

Countless Bethlehem families are adjusting to the hard, painful reality. For Richard Lynn, who worked his way up to a Bethlehem Steel foreman, this is particularly wrenching. Five generations of the Lynn family had worked at Bethlehem Steel, most of them starting at the mill as soon as they came of age. Now it seems certain he will be the last of the line. His father has recently retired, and his brother Tom was laid off in 1983 and never called back. Richard sees workers with twenty years of seniority being bumped back to jobs as laborers in the beam yard, which used to be an entry-level position. What hope then for the next generation?

"It's just survival now," Lynn says. "So I told my boys, 'You better get an education because there's not going to be a job like I had or your grandfather had. We're not sure there's going to be a Bethlehem Steel Company.'"

For Donald H. Trautlein, chairman of Bethlehem Steel, and his team of would-be corporate rescuers who had been trying to reverse the trend, the grimness they saw around them was compounded. Despite the anguish of dismissing many loyal employees, closing once-productive plants, and disrupting entire communities, Bethlehem Steel lost $2.1 billion in five straight years of red ink from 1982 through 1986. The Trautlein team could not restore profitability even as they slashed the company's total workforce from eighty thousand in 1981 to about thirty-five thousand at the end of 1986. Now Bethlehem is selling its profitable subsidiaries, including Kusan, a plastics firm, and J. M. Tull Industries, a steel service center, in a desperate move to buy more time to save the steel company.

Bitterly disappointed, Trautlein conceded in mid-February of 1986 that he had reached the end of the line. Abruptly, the company announced that he was surrendering his authority as chief executive officer. While remaining as chairman for a few more months, Trautlein, on May 31, 1986, turned over all operations to Walter L. Williams, 57, the company president, who also assumed the chairmanship.

Trautlein, the cost cutter, had reached a limit in both his strategic plan and his patience. He had hoped to step out either after reporting a profitable quarter or after turning 60 in August of 1986. However, when he and four other chief executives of the nation's largest steel mills met in Pittsburgh early in the year with Lynn Williams, Trautlein became enraged at what he regarded as Williams's intransigence. Reflecting subsequently on his uncharacteristic outburst at the union leader, Trautlein decided someone else should try to move the unmovable.

"I sincerely regret that the environment in which we have operated over the past four years has been so harsh," he said in stepping aside. "The toll on Bethlehem Steel Corporation, our employees, their families and communities has been awesome. To my knowledge, at the beginning of this decade no one, inside or outside the industry, foresaw that the economic conditions facing the industry would be as adverse as they ultimately turned out to be. . . .

"The actions of management in a basic industry such as steel, where planning and investment cycles are so long, can only be measured in terms of hindsight," he continued. "Time will judge the effectiveness of the strategic decisions made by Bethlehem during my term as chief executive officer."

Bethlehem's future is now in the hands of Walter F. Williams, a thirty-five-year employee who rose from the ranks. As a former chief engineer of construction, he was a familiar figure among blue-collar workers.

Williams once did the unheard of by participating in a union-sponsored debate attended by seventy-five top labor leaders. There he stressed that all of basic industry was in trouble and only labor's cooperation could save it. That set off the following exchange:

"Walt, you are asking us to lower our standard of living, aren't you?" one union leader asked.

"Yes," Williams replied.

"You are asking us to live like some of the low-wage foreign producers?" another persisted.

"No," Williams said. "I'm not asking you to live like a Korean steelworker. I am asking you to get down to a level a little closer to the wages paid for manufacturing in America."

Bethlehem Steel's unyielding problems epitomize the serious trouble that has beset the entire industry.

As conditions worsened, more than twenty steel firms disappeared from the marketplace or filed for protection under Chapter 11 of the bankruptcy laws. Well-known firms like Youngstown Sheet and Tube, Alan Wood, and Wisconsin are gone. At mid-July 1986, LTV, the nation's second largest steelmaker since its merger with Republic Steel in 1984, sought Chapter 11 protection, following Wheeling-Pittsburgh, another top-ten steelmaker, which filed for it some months earlier. And the steel companies that survive have been unable to reverse the revenue drain that started in 1982, their total losses exceeding $8 billion by the end of 1986, according to American Iron and Steel Institute figures.

Are we witnessing the deindustrialization of America, as some economists contend? Or are these extraordinary shock waves from changes in our basic industrial fabric that must be confronted for the sake of our stability and security? If steel was once so important to our national interest that President Truman seized the mills and at least three other presidents directly intervened to halt steel strikes, can it be much less crucial to us today? And if big steel is still important, what will save it?

I posed these questions to dozens of leaders of industry, labor, and academe. If there is no consensus, they nevertheless expressed strong views about steel's future.

At one end of the spectrum, M. Colyer Crum of the Harvard Business School views big steel's demise as inevitable. Back in May of 1979, at a time when the prevailing wisdom among steel economists was that the signs of distress were temporary, Crum diagnosed them as terminal. He shocked many observers by declaring that Bethlehem Steel was on the same course that killed the Penn Central Railroad.

Crum's judgment, given in a speech at a meeting of the Young President's Organization in Rio De Janeiro, swiftly became known throughout the industry.

Crum recalls that someone from Bethlehem Steel called even before he returned from Rio, leaving the message, "Would you give another speech and tell us the solutions?" With some chagrin, he replied, "You can't change anything until you guys get the message of what I tried to say in Rio. Which is, the decline is intractable, it's long term, and there is no quick fix. If you tell me you want another speech with solutions, you don't understand the first speech."

Crum's projections were, of course, starkly on target. Has anything changed to moderate his grim outlook?

"The Penn Central went under because the pay was too high and the work rules too rigid, and a lot of its track went to the wrong places," he says. "That's [the situation] in steel. They are stuck with factories that are now in the wrong places, but they can't change them. If you have a mill with no growth in America, it is going to be old mill. If [you] build a new mill, which is in the right place, then investors are not going to hold shares in Bethlehem Steel. That's the simple message from an outsider who neither knows nor cares about details."

The search for an expert who speaks from the perspective of studying steel industry details leads to the campus of Fordham University in New York City. This is the base of the Reverend William T. Hogan, S.J., who is probably the most prolific writer and lecturer on the state of the steel industry. Not surprisingly, he views its future far more positively.

Father Hogan likes the way steel firms have been closing marginal facilities and cutting costs. He also sees a lifeline for the industry in President Reagan's program to negotiate voluntary quotas with the goal of restricting steel imports to 18.5 percent of the domestic market.

"Note that the tonnage that has been taken out—the 21 million capacity that has been lost since 1980—was mostly obsolete stuff," Father Hogan points out. "That means what is left is more competitive than what the industry had five years ago . . . and every major company now has under construction, or finishing construction, a continuous casting unit. That is going to make all of the industry more efficient.

"The aim of some of the companies is to get down to four man-hours per ton of steel. The industry will have 60 to 85 percent of its tonnage continuous cast. [Japan attained a 90 percent average about five years ago.] So you will have a smaller industry operating with better equipment.

"The import restrictions will give the industry about six or seven million more tons a year, providing this 18.5 percent limit is achieved," he continues. "The integrated mills should pick up a big chunk of the tonnage and another thing [the quotas] will do is stabilize the price structure."

By the time the five-year protection period expires, the

industry can expect to see markets expanding again, according to the Hogan projections.

"The industry is not going to die. There may be some change in the structure, but you got something like 4 billion people-plus now and by the year 2000 demographers seem sure there will be something like 6 billion people. And by the year 2020 you will have something like 8 billion people. The point is those people cannot live without an infrastructure. And infrastructure is going to demand a fair amount of steel. So I think there is growth ahead for steel. It is not next year or the year after, but by the 1990s you will see some change."

In Charlotte, North Carolina, F. Kenneth Iverson is uncomfortable with both views. As chairman of Nucor, he is the chief executive officer of seven minimills that operate on four sites. His company has returned a steady profit and no employees have been laid off, largely because his high-technology, nonunion, profit-sharing mills invaded the traditional markets of integrated steel and even competed successfully against price-cutting imports.

Iverson insists the steel business must be viewed from a global perspective. He resents Big Steel's penchant for looking to Washington for salvation.

"The import-protection program forced on the Reagan administration will hurt the American steel markets in the long run," he says. "Because quotas are designed to protect higher-priced American steel, [they] will force U.S. manufacturers to 'source' outside the U.S. That means U.S. companies who make oil rigs, or autos, or tractors will ship in parts and components from abroad to avoid higher steel prices domestically, thus circumventing the quota system, which applies only to raw steel.

"If the market for American steel decreases because of that, the entire steel industry suffers and so does the U.S. economy," he says. "Ironically, we will end up with a smaller steel market, making us shut down even further—which is the very thing quotas are designed to prevent."

Iverson declares integrated steel companies can help

themselves best by working to reverse "bad decisions" made in the 1950s and 1960s. "Labor costs ran out of control. I'm not talking about dollars per hour . . . I'm talking about manning. The main problem is the productivity, and that's related to [workers] not being technically up to date and also to featherbedding—and here I include administrative and clerical people who are just as bad as the blue-collar worker."

With current technology, minimills can produce only about 30 percent of the nation's steel. That will go higher, in time, Iverson says, but this leaves integrated mills with a decent future if they improve on what they do best— manufacturing the big structurals, the larger pipes, and the great amounts of flat-rolled products needed for autos and appliances.

"But they have far too many people who are in their pocket," he says. "I mean, you got six guys on the furnace instead of three. That doubles your costs. You can cut your costs 10 percent but you really haven't cut your costs that much because you are not producing. An illustration: the average integrated mill produces about 350 tons per employee. The average Japanese mill now produces about 800 tons per employee. To get from that 350 to 800 you have cut [costs] in half. Well, you can't do that. The most you can cut is 20 percent so that means that most of that has to come from better productivity."

Iverson believes American mills can match or exceed the Japanese performance, given the latter's transportation disadvantage. He points out that a big reason some of his own plants do is because they are not burdened by work rules that the big companies granted during years of industry-wide bargaining.

The integrated steel industry must shed archaic practices if it is to survive, Iverson declares. "You have to tell the union members that it is not in their best interests to lose their jobs. That shouldn't be too difficult now after four straight years of losses. It's in [the workers'] best interest for the company to succeed. In order to get them [to cooperate] you have to do a little sharing along the way—of problems and profits."

Everything I found in my research supports the Iverson assessment. High wages are not the problem in the steel industry: ossified, union-dictated work practices are the problem.

The debilitating work rules are, of course, those based on past practices regarding crew sizes and craft jurisdictions going back to 1956, and under the industry-wide contract, they could not be changed except when new processes were installed. Since so few innovations have been adopted by capital-strapped American industry, inviolate contract provisions have frozen the big steel plants in time. Meanwhile, foreign competitors and American minimills are constantly adapting their labor practices.

Carnegie would shudder today if he could see what this rigidity has done to his enlightened concept of an integrated steel industry. Steel has reverted to a cottage industry, replete with all of the inefficiencies that made previous cottage industries ripe for extinction. In a typical steelmaking shop, there are more than twenty different crafts and job classes, each with a defined jurisdiction and each with restrictions that spell out limits of involvement in the steelmaking process. No worker is allowed to do any task outside his narrow job description, even in a prolonged lull on his own job. The industry has locked itself into a position that Robert Crandall, the Brookings Institution economist, publicly refers to as untenable—and terminal. "If steel expects to keep wages 70 percent above the industrial average and work rules where only 60 to 70 percent is productive, that's a prescription for disappearing," he says.

If Lynn Williams is, indeed, the rising labor leader of the future, he must see death marching on the American steel industry. Yet, even as the times cry for mutual inventiveness, Williams agrees to no such moves.

While agreeing to modest wage concessions, the international union adamantly fought off demands for changes in past work practices in the company-by-company bargaining that was reinstated in 1986. Only the USX Corporation, the

nation's largest steel producer, won master contract concessions on those critical issues, but at the price of a costly,
record-setting confrontation with the union.

USX refused to extend its contract when it expired on
August 1, 1986, giving notice that it was determined to obtain
relief from the archaic work rules, the restrictive job classifications, and the contracting-out restraints that have been punishing the industry for the last thirty years. That set off a
184-day work stoppage which was described as a "strike" by
the company and a "lockout" by the union.

The company finally won the right to reduce manning by
combining its more than twenty-plus crafts into eight at most
plants and even six at others. Further, the new agreement
permits it for the first time to assign craftsmen to operate
certain equipment and allow operations workers to perform
minor repairs that were once exclusively handled by the
crafts. But it was a costly settlement, achieved only because
USX had maintained a fully funded pension plan—which no
other steel company had—and, in effect, was able to buy the
right to cut out jobs with two-for-one pensions. (In eliminating three hundred jobs, for example, the company provides
six hundred pensions—three hundred for the terminated employees and three hundred for others who agree to take early
retirement voluntarily, providing they got the same $400-a-
month supplement that is added to pensions of terminated
employees. The company is then obligated to fill the latter
three hundred vacancies by recalling employees on layoff.)

The new contract provides a flexibility that puts USX in
the driver's seat once the money from the record work stoppage is recouped. What is to become of the remainder of the
big steel producers, the firms that do not have the resources
to weather a prolonged work stoppage or buy that flexibility
with a costly dip into pension funds? If the American steel
industry is to compete in global markets, it must undergo a
plant-by-plant restructuring to modernize, phase out old
plants, and increase productivity by reducing man-hours per
ton.

Their options for survival become increasingly grim. Unless management and labor start working in tandem to make their plants free of death-inducing work practices and forego costly confrontations such as the one that closed USX plants for half a year, a new surge of filings for protection from bankruptcy is inevitable. The companies' hope of survival then dwindles to cutting costs by throwing the burden of their pension funds upon the government—a practice that is causing much national unease. When LTV filed for Chapter 11 protection, it unloaded its four debt-ridden pension plans upon the Pension Benefits Guarantee Corporation, the federal agency that guarantees pensions for all American workers. Steelworkers on early retirement promptly lost their $400-a-month retirement bonuses because the PBGC ruled that they exceeded its limits. Now, with other big steel firms on the brink of Chapter 11, the very liquidity of the PBGC has become a concern in Congress, raising real questions of whether the drain from steel will affect pension protections for workers in other sectors of the troubled American economy.

I believe the changes needed to restore health to the steel industry cannot be negotiated in a single contract nor come from concessions forced by the courts in Chapter 11 proceedings. They must evolve out of an era of adjustment and change that can come only from a mutual determination to save the industry.

It will take a fundamental gut change from the top to the bottom—from the loftiest management thinker to the lowliest blue-collar toiler—to launch such an effort, but there is encouraging precedent showing it can be done.

The auto industry, forced to consider its own survival because of foreign competition, chucked old adversarial roles and made imaginative breakthroughs, thanks to the joint work of the United Automobile Workers and the Big Three auto companies. For example, job classifications at the joint General Motors and Toyota venture at Fremont, California, were cut from eighty to four to make operations more flexible and better to utilize the talents of workers.

Lynn Williams states that "concessions are behind us" in the steel industry. The fact is, they haven't begun. Williams must recognize this, sell his board on it and, indeed, carry the message to all local steelworker officials. Not only are jobs at stake, but the LTV example should be lesson enough to show that the hard-earned pensions of many thousands of retired steelworkers are in jeopardy. This is the ultimate test of Williams's leadership. Whether he summons the courage will determine whether he will be the bright union leader who saves the industry—or the union boss who buries it.

However, Walter Williams and the other steel company executives must be ready with concessions of equal magnitude. For the right to run their companies efficiently again, the industry must help retrain their displaced employees, just as the auto industry has done. Instead of just the traditional wage packages, the industry also must offer employees equity through profit sharing and stock awards. And most fundamental of all, it must give workers a genuine involvement at every level from the shop floor to, yes, the sacrosanct steel-company boardroom. A labor member on the Bethlehem Steel board might cause tremors at Eugene Grace's Nisky Hill gravesite, but it would show the company is serious about making amends for decades of ignoring the creativity of its workers. It is important, too, that steel company top executives avoid the bad public perceptions created by "golden parachutes" and other financial windfalls for themselves, as they call for sacrifices from the workers.

Finally, President Reagan has an opportunity to hasten this transition. He missed a chance in 1984 to exact strong commitments from the industry and union to improve efficiency in exchange for voluntary import restraints. Now that both management and labor are demanding intensified enforcement to meet the 18.5 percent quota goal, Reagan again has the opportunity to ask what progress the steel industry is making in helping itself.

The nation needs a viable steel industry. I believe the public falsely assumes that we will always have one. While great debates have raged over the cost of the defense budget, aid to Contras, and other national security issues, we have all but ignored the past two decades of steady decline in our industrial base, which adversely affects the defense capability of our nation. Minimills could not ever supply the country's basic steel needs, and it would be folly to depend on foreign steel. Once the steel plants go down, no amount of shouting through bullhorns or demands for legislation against steel closings will revive them. The public should be aware of this. The time to use those bullhorns is now. It is in everyone's interest to insist that the American steel industry stop killing itself.

Index

C